D1116736

BEYOND REPAIR

BEYOND REPAIR

The Decline *and* Fall *of the* CIA

Charles S. Faddis

LYONS PRESS
Guilford, Connecticut
An Imprint of Globe Pequot Press

All statements of fact, opinion, or analysis expressed are those of the author and do not reflect the official positions or views of the CIA or any other U.S. Government agency. Nothing in the contents should be construed as asserting or implying U.S. Government authentication of information or Agency endorsement of the author's views. This material has been reviewed by the CIA to prevent the disclosure of classified information.

Lyons Press is an imprint of Globe Pequot Press.

Library of Congress Cataloging-in-Publication Data is available on file.

ISBN 978-1-59921-851-9

Printed in the United States of America

10 9 8 7 6 5 4 3 2 1

Contents

To the men and women of the Clandestine Service, out there now as they have been for sixty years, on the ridgetops, in the back alleys, hunting the monsters the world prefers to pretend do not exist.

Acknowledgments

With apologies in advance to all those I am inevitably going to omit, here are a few of the individuals without whom this manuscript could never have been completed.

First, I want to thank my wife, Gina. She has been the love of my life for thirty-plus years, and it is no exaggeration to say that without her there never would have been a book. They say that we are born as halves of complete individuals and that when you find your soul mate only then do you become whole. I can tell you that is true, and that I am one of the lucky ones who found the rest of himself.

Next, I want to thank my kids, Hannah, Tucker, Libby, and Ike. Sometimes they proofread copy. Sometimes they did research. Sometimes they just cooked dinner, so Dad could keep writing. Regardless, they were indispensable and, as always, my inspiration.

There are a host of current and former intelligence officers and special ops folks I would like to thank as well. They have provided wise counsel. They have told me when I was on the right track and when I was lost. Many, in years past, have kept me alive. I will name only a handful here. Hans, Happy, Dakota, Reaper, Fury, Joe, Snake, Sasquatch, Doogie, Boomerang, Mr. Wizard, Maffu, Pix, Gary, Sipowitz—thank you.

Outside the community there are another vast number of people who have been instrumental in the drafting of this work. Some of them have provided deep philosophical insights. Some have reminded me how to use a spell checker and called my attention to that fact that "normal" people do not necessarily know what MASINT is. Again, I will name only a few. Bud, Karl, Miss Pat, Jeffrey, Patty, John—thank you.

And, finally, I need to express my deep appreciation to Hawk, who walked point. "Every man dies; not every man truly lives," Hawk. Keep the faith.

Charles S. Faddis

Introduction

LET ME START BY SAYING WHAT THIS BOOK IS NOT.

It is not an attack on the men and women of the Clandestine Service of the Central Intelligence Agency, the overwhelming majority of whom are dedicated, patriotic Americans working hard every day on behalf of their fellow citizens. God knows that they do not do it for the money nor do they do it for the recognition. They do it because they believe in the work and because they know, as I do, that there really are monsters in the world, and someone has to protect us from them.

It is also not an argument against the existence of a central human intelligence collection organization within the United States government. We desperately needed a central intelligence agency in 1947, when the CIA was created. We even more desperately need such an entity today. The threats facing us are multiplying and becoming more complex. The time horizons in which threats are emerging are shortening. Technology is evolving at an astonishing rate, and we are fast approaching the day when there will be dozens of groups and nations on this planet capable of threatening us with biological, chemical, radiological, and nuclear weapons. This is not pulp fiction. This is reality.

This book is an argument that the existing Central Intelligence Agency is no longer capable of performing the task for which it was designed and must, rapidly, be replaced.

Somewhere out there in the ether right now a terrorist organization is working hard on an anthrax program with the express goal of launching a biological attack on the United States of America. Such an attack, with even a moderate amount of the bacteria, if properly executed, could, without the use of any sophisticated technology, kill tens of thousands and force the evacuation of major American cities.

Several nations in the world, despite our best diplomatic efforts, have already succeeded in acquiring nuclear weapons. These include not just traditional powers such as Russia and China but also much less stable and predictable nations, such as

Pakistan, India, and North Korea. Proliferation is real, and the threat is expanding. For all its dangers the Cold War was characterized by a great degree of predictability. Both the United States and the Soviet Union had in place elaborate command-and-control structures and could be counted on to act very deliberately and with due regard for long-term strategic interests.

The same cannot be said of the nations now fielding nuclear arms. A friend of mine used to say of the challenge of determining what India's nuclear war plans were, that it was complicated by the fact that the Indians themselves did not know. Pakistan, which is engaged eyeball to eyeball with India in a nuclear standoff, is an even more fragile and unpredictable entity. The prospects for an actual exchange of nuclear weapons in the subcontinent in the next ten to twenty years are enormous. The consequences for all of humanity would be almost unimaginable. These are nations with huge populations, where hundreds of millions of individuals wrestle with poverty and disease on a daily basis. The aftermath of a nuclear war between India and Pakistan would probably most resemble the Dark Ages, and the survival of either nation as a viable entity in its wake would be problematic at best.

Russia has not gone away. The Russians are a great and proud people. I have known many, even some who were adversaries, over the years, whom I count as good friends. This does not mean that their national interests coincide with ours. They are rebuilding, and they are working to reassert themselves in areas of the world that they consider crucial to their national interests. They remain the second most powerful nation on earth, after the United States, in military terms. The nature of the government in Moscow, its plans and intentions, and the security of its nuclear arsenal are still of vital importance to our nation.

The Chinese are not our friends. It may or may not be a good thing that we can all go to Wal-Mart and buy televisions and DVD players at a fraction of the cost they would be if they were still produced in the United States. Regardless, it remains true that China is a Communist nation, that it denies basic human rights to its citizens, that it supports North Korea, that it is engaged in a massive military buildup, and that its explosive economic growth is placing its entire political, economic, and social structure under almost incalculable strain. We may find ourselves at war with China in ten years; we may witness a second Chinese Revolution in ten years. Regardless of what happens, given China's size, its economic and military power, and its geographic position, anything that occurs regarding it will have huge ramifications worldwide.

Obviously, I could continue with a list of threats and challenges almost ad infinitum. I have said nothing about the implications of Hugo Chavez, an implacable foe of the United States, controlling Venezuela's oil supplies; of Iran's backing for Hizbullah; or of drug cartels in Mexico becoming so powerful as to begin to challenge the Mexican army itself to open, armed confrontation. The examples I have touched upon were selected simply to provide a flavor of the complexity and the severity of the threats that we face.

There are a lot of mechanisms for the collection of intelligence, and a great deal of it can be collected openly. We are a long way from the days when an operative might be sent to Vladivostok to acquire maps of shipping channels or cable home general atmospherics. A huge amount of information is openly available in print and on the Internet. This can and should be exploited.

There are other extremely valuable ways to collect intelligence. Massive amounts of information can be sucked off the airwaves, stolen from e-mail communications, or gleaned from imagery. This is being done and obviously must continue. SIGINT, ELINT, IMINT, MASINT, and others, are all crucial to our national security.

That said, at the end of the day, there are key things that only HUMINT is going to tell you. Imagery and signals intelligence may give you a very good picture of the movement of Russian forces toward the border of the former Soviet Republic of Georgia in the wake of Russian accusations that the Georgians unjustly arrested and incarcerated Russian citizens in Tbilisi. Only human intelligence is going to tell you what the president and prime minister of Russia discussed regarding this crisis in the meeting that took place last night. Only human intelligence is going to tell you whether the deployment of forces is intended as a bluff to secure political concessions or is, in fact, a precursor to war.

In 1941 the Soviet Union was invaded by Nazi Germany. The initial stages of the war were a disaster for the Russians, who were caught by surprise and rapidly overrun. By the time the Russian winter intervened to tip the scales, the Germans were literally at the gates of Moscow.

Surprise? The invading force numbered in the millions. The movement of men and material to the border had been ongoing for months. Even without satellites or other modern technical means, there was no way that the Soviets could not have been aware of the buildup. Everyone living within a hundred miles of the border in Poland could see firsthand what was unfolding.

And yet the Russians were surprised. They were surprised because they believed the buildup was a bluff done for political reasons. They had convinced themselves that the Germans would not attack, and they lacked the necessary human intelligence that would have told them that an invasion was imminent. The growth in the scope and capability of electronic forms of intelligence collection between the Second World War and today has not changed this calculus. The only way we are going to know the plans and intentions of our adversaries is by the use of well-placed human sources.

On May 11, 1998, the Indian government detonated three nuclear devices simultaneously at the Pokhran test range in western India. The Indian government did not announce its intention to detonate these devices in advance, and the United States received no warning from any source of intelligence regarding the impending detonations, despite the fact that the Indian nuclear program had been a focus of collection for decades. We were caught flat-footed.

The test range in question is located in an area of flat desert where the air is clear most of the year. The location of the range is known and has been known for many years. The movement of nuclear devices, scientists, and technicians to a range of this type in advance of a test is not something that can be done overnight. It requires careful preparation over a period of weeks, if not months, and involves the assembly at the range of individuals and items coming from all over India. It would be hard to think of a better target for technical collection. Certainly, it is difficult to imagine that such tests could be conducted without someone's seeing something on imagery or someone's noting message traffic regarding the movement of key scientific personnel.

And yet the United States was surprised and fundamentally for the same reasons that the Soviet Union was surprised when half the German army started its tank engines one morning and launched an invasion. The problem was lack of human sources in the right positions to provide the required intelligence. No one told Stalin what Hitler's plan was. No one told the United States that the Indians intended to conduct their first full-scale nuclear tests since 1974.

Unfortunately, the situation has not improved for the United States in this regard. Despite herculean and often heroic efforts on the part of many individuals within the Central Intelligence Agency, we continue to suffer a series of failures that demonstrate that we are not recruiting and running the key sources we need to provide warning of threats to our nation.

On September 11, 2001, three airliners crashed into targets in the United States. Two hit the World Trade Center. One hit the Pentagon. A fourth crashed in Pennsylvania instead of Washington only because a group of men and women with almost unbelievable courage decided to take matters into their own hands. We spend billions on defense and intel collection, yet it came down to the passengers and crew on a civilian airliner to save the U.S. Capitol building from destruction.

A lot has been written about September 11. Many hundreds, if not thousands, of pages have been written about lessons learned. They are many. A lot of people, in a lot of organizations, contributed to this debacle. Many organizations within the United States government share the responsibility for the loss of life.

That said, first and foremost, September 11 was a failure in collection, and the organization most responsible for that failure was the CIA. The Central Intelligence Agency was created in 1947 for the express purpose of ensuring that we would never again suffer another Pearl Harbor, that we would never again be surprised by an adversary and forced to suffer the kind of losses and humiliation we did on December 7, 1941.

A little less than sixty years after Pearl Harbor, despite all the resources at its disposal, the CIA, and, more specifically, the

Directorate of Operations within the CIA, failed in that responsibility. We lost three thousand American lives to a sneak attack on American soil. And frankly, the defeat was made that much more humiliating and incomprehensible because we were assaulted not by the armed might of Imperial Japan but by a small group of fanatics using box cutters as weapons.

In the summer of 2002, I took the first CIA team into northern Iraq in preparation for the pending invasion. I remained on the ground there in command of a CIA team for roughly the next year. Prior to the insertion of my team, we were briefed at length on a variety of subjects, including the CIA's assessment of the status of Iraq's weapons of mass destruction (WMD) programs. The overall scope of that assessment is now public record. While there was some dispute on a few issues, it was accepted that Saddam was continuing a variety of programs and was in possession of at least some quantity of chemical and biological agents.

During our time in Iraq, our team devoted a great deal of energy to the effort to acquire intelligence on WMD programs. This was not our central focus; the decision to go to war had already been made, but it was definitely on our list of targets to work. We never acquired intelligence confirming the assessment that had been given to us prior to our insertion. We never assumed handling of a single existing Iraqi asset. Every source we ran we recruited after we went in country.

As time passed, and as we continued to see the comments coming out of Washington, it became increasingly puzzling to us as to what sources of information were being used to form the assessment that Saddam had WMD. We were the only people inside the country. We weren't telling anyone that we had conclusive evidence of the existence of such weapons, and we were unaware of the existence of any assets that were on the books before we went in country that had access to Iraqi WMD programs. So who was it that was telling the Bush administration that Saddam had the programs in question?

A full exploration of this topic is beyond the scope of this book and has been discussed, in any event, in many other places by individuals much more informed on the topic than I am. Let it suffice to say what we all already know: The WMD programs did not exist. Our assessments were wrong. Once again, despite the most capable technical intelligence collection systems on the planet, we were caught without the information we needed to make critical national security decisions. Perhaps we should have invaded Iraq anyway. It is certainly a great and wonderful thing that Saddam is gone. No matter what, though, we should not have been in the position of basing our decision upon faulty intelligence.

Let me come back to my original point. The failure of the CIA to collect the intelligence we needed in advance of September 11 is not the consequence of sloth or lack of dedication on the part of the workforce of that organization. We talk a lot these days about the "war on terror" and people that are on the "front lines" in that fight. I'm not sure exactly what all that means or where the front lines are, but I can tell you that the men and women of the Directorate of Operations of the CIA are way out beyond those frontlines, operating deep in enemy territory. They are out there every day, with very little support and no backup, putting their lives on the line for mediocre pay and limited, if any, recognition. And increasingly these days, the thanks they get from this nation for doing the dangerous work they do is to be subjected to investigation and insult. Every senior officer I know in the CIA carries personal liability insurance, because of the fear of being sued for actions taken in the line of duty.

The failure of the CIA is structural. The machine is broken, and it is broken beyond repair. It does not need mending; it needs replacing, and we need to move quickly in doing so before we discover that the next attack on American soil is an improvised nuclear device going off on the docks in New Jersey or the introduction of bubonic plague into a major city.

There are many factors that have contributed to the breakdown in the performance of the CIA. Some of them are internal. Many of them are not. The purpose of this book is to identify and explain those factors and then to lay out a roadmap for how, I believe, they can be addressed. The goal remains the same as it was in 1947—to create an entity that will maintain the midnight watch, so Americans can sleep well at night.

CHAPTER ONE

Donovan Would Not Make It

THE FOUNDER OF THE OFFICE OF STRATEGIC SERVICES (OSS) IN World War II was William J. (Wild Bill) Donovan. During action against the Germans in World War I, Donovan took a machine-gun bullet to the knee. He refused to be evacuated, insisting instead on remaining on the field, leading the men under his command in an assault on German positions. His actions on that date won him the nation's highest military honor, the Medal of Honor. By the end of the war, he had added three Purple Hearts, the Distinguished Service Cross, the Distinguished Service Medal, and a number of foreign decorations as well, making him one of the most highly decorated Americans of the war.[1]

After the First World War, Donovan visited Europe, Siberia, and Japan. He became a Wall Street lawyer, assistant U.S. attorney general, and business executive. In 1935 he toured Italian battle lines in Ethiopia.[2] Beginning in 1940 he made a series of trips on behalf of President Franklin Delano Roosevelt to Britain, the Balkans, and the Mediterranean to gather information on the state of hostilities, Britain's staying power, and how to improve American intelligence and covert-action capabilities. He created the Coordinator of Information (COI) in July 1941, America's first peacetime national intelligence organization. In June 1942 this group would be renamed the Office of Strategic Services (OSS).[3]

Donovan went ashore on the first day of the invasion of Sicily, advancing alongside the First Infantry Division and personally engaging enemy troops with a machine gun.[4] Against the express orders of the Secretary of the Navy, Donovan also personally participated in the Normandy landings, at one point being pinned down by enemy fire.[5] On one occasion he smuggled a silenced pistol into the Oval Office and discharged it into a sandbag behind the back of the president, as a demonstration of the effectiveness of the silencing mechanism.[6] During a visit to Detachment 101, the OSS unit assigned to the Burmese theater, Donovan infiltrated 150 miles behind Japanese lines in an antique biplane flown by 101's commanding officer. His purpose was to visit an OSS forward operating base and meet directly with Kachin Hills tribe leaders.[7]

Donovan recruited to the OSS a wide cross section of America, searching for the best and the brightest but also those with exceptional creativity and daring. OSS wanted "out of the box" thinkers—individuals who were unorthodox, brilliant, perhaps even eccentric. Recruits included Ivy League professors, safecrackers, former Communists who had fought in the Spanish Civil War, professional baseball players, actors, and paratroopers. They were all, in the words of Donovan, his "glorious amateurs," and they lived by the same mantra he did: "If you fall, fall forward."[8]

Donovan would not make it in the CIA today. He would be branded as too aggressive, a "cowboy," and someone lacking the requisite "corporate" attitude. He would in due course, if he decided to stick it out, find himself riding a desk somewhere in a corner at headquarters, shelved, put someplace where he "couldn't do any harm." His performance evaluations would include the liberal use of such terms as "aggressive" and "forward leaning" and "singular focus on mission accomplishment," which in today's CIA are not compliments. They mean an officer puts the mission above bureaucracy and groupthink, and that is the kiss of death.

Not long before I retired from the CIA, I was having a conversation with a friend and fellow CIA officer about Gary Berntsen, the leader of the Jawbreaker team during the American invasion of Afghanistan. I know Gary only in passing. He and I never served together, but I have read his book, and I know the background of the events described therein. I asked my friend if he had read Gary's book, and when he said no, I offered to lend him a copy.

My friend thanked me for the offer but declined to take the book. He then went on to say that while we, meaning the CIA, needed to have a "few Garys around" to take care of unpleasant business when necessary, Gary did not really have what it took to make it in the organization as a senior officer and did not represent what we wanted in our senior ranks. Accordingly, my friend did not feel that it was worth his time to read Gary's comments about opportunities missed in Afghanistan.

I was floored.

I am not sure I would recognize Gary if he walked into the room. He and I may have met on a few occasions, but as noted above, to my recollection we never served together. I have no personal reason for supporting anything he says, but how in the world can we seriously say that individuals like Gary Berntsen do not have what we need for today's CIA?

This is a guy who voluntarily left his post as chief of station in Latin America and took charge of a team being sent into a dangerous and fluid situation at a time of national crisis. His leadership of that team was brilliant. Under his command his men accomplished everything they were tasked to do and more. Former president George W. Bush was fond of saying things about "hunting people to the ends of the earth" and "smoking them out of their holes." Well, Jawbreaker actually did that.

I had a member of the Jawbreaker team, Dakota, on my team later in Iraq. He was a Marine scout-sniper before he joined the CIA and is a tough guy, not prone to hyperbole or gratuitous compliments. He described Gary as a "stud" and talked with awe about the purpose and drive and leadership he brought to the fight against al-Qaeda in Afghanistan. He had no doubt that if the Bush administration had made military forces available as requested bin Laden would have been killed or captured right there and then at Tora Bora.[9]

The man responsible for this success is not the kind of man we want in a senior leadership position at CIA? Why not? Because he has a tendency to speak truth to power and to put mission accomplishment ahead of bureaucratic interests? Whom then do we want to run the CIA, and what attributes should they have? Donovan craved independence and initiative. He said, "I'd rather have a young lieutenant with guts enough to disobey an order than a colonel too regimented to think and act for himself."[10] What happened to that spirit?

In the mid-1990s I had a series of meetings in the Middle East with an official from a terrorist organization who was considering volunteering his services to the CIA. They were difficult, protracted discussions filled with a lot of back-and-forth and a lot of soul searching on the part of the individual with whom I met. He was no friend of the United States: He had spent the better part of his adult life engaged in a war against the West in general and America in particular. Our nation, in his view, represented a threat to the very existence of the Muslim world and the culture in which he had been born and raised.

When I met with him, this individual had not moderated these original views to any great extent. He had, however, through personal experience in combat, come to be quite disillusioned with terrorist tactics and with the use of violence to further political goals in general. He was still a long way from being a friend of ours, but he had seen enough killing. There was room for common ground, for an accommodation.

At the conclusion of days of meetings, the individual in question and I had reached an understanding. We would cooperate for the purpose of preventing loss of life. He was en route to a new country, and he would meet with us there to provide information. He agreed to accept money from us, in limited quantities, while making clear that he would never agree to be "paid" and that he would take only what was just as compensation for expenses he incurred on our behalf. It was one of those critical moments when all the hazards and challenges of my career seemed to pale in comparison with the potential rewards. This man, in our employ, could save lives, thwart attacks, and lead us to targets for whom we had been searching for many years.

I was ordered to break contact with that terrorist official. I was told that he was a citizen of a nation with whom we had friendly relations. It was assessed that if we were caught in contact with this individual the possible damage to our political relations with the country in question would be significant. The calculation was that it was more important to ensure that there was no possibility of a problem with our liaison relationship than it was to run a relatively senior source within this terrorist group. The priority was avoiding a "flap" by not penetrating this terrorist organization.

Based on this direction, and after arguing the point long and hard, I met with the official and advised that we would not be establishing a relationship with him. It was, not surprisingly, a surreal conversation. I sat across the table from a man who had just spent days working out in his own mind how he could rationalize helping us against his own comrades and how he could help us save the lives of American citizens, and I had to tell him we were not interested in working with him. I suspect he walked out the door at the end of that meeting thinking that we deserved what was coming, that if we were not willing to lift a hand to defend ourselves, we probably should be destroyed.

The chief of station who instructed me to break contact was probably the single best chief for whom I ever worked. He had been in government service all his life, beginning with multiple combat tours in Vietnam. He did not tell me to walk away from the case because he didn't care. He did not tell me to walk away because he didn't understand what this source could do for us. He did it because he knew what headquarters would and would not support. He knew that no one was pressuring him to recruit terrorist sources. He knew that no one was going to stand behind him if he ran a high-risk op and it went bad. He understood that he was working without a net.

Donovan said, "If you fall, fall forward." That had now become "Don't fall."

A few years ago, in a brief before an operation, I listened while the officer under my command who was running the op briefed the personnel involved. He concluded his remarks by saying something to the effect of "Remember, you may have to improvise. Anytime you go out on the street, something could go wrong."

The officer meant this comment as an eye-opener, a reminder to junior personnel that things do not always go as well in real life as they do in training. The comments were fine as far as they went, but I didn't think they went far enough.

"Forget about the idea that things *may* go wrong," I said. "Things *will* go wrong. Guaranteed. From the moment you hit the street, you will have to begin to modify your plan accordingly. Sometimes the problems will be minor. Sometimes they will be significant. Sometimes they will wreck your whole day. If you cannot accept that, don't get out of bed in the morning. Pull the covers over your head, and stay where it's safe."

I don't cite the examples above for the purpose of highlighting any particular contribution I may or may not have made during my career; I use them for the purpose of illustration only. I have no reason to think that the official with whom I met would have helped us avoid the attacks of September 11, 2001, although he may, in fact, have been involved in the run-up to other operations. What's important is that there is nothing unique or special about these events. Every CIA ops officer who is worth his or her salt has had a myriad of similar experiences and has been prevented by political climate and bureaucracy from doing what has to be done. As demonstrated by the decision in 1998 to walk away from the attack on bin Ladin's Tarnak Farms compound, we have let a lot of targets get away over the years, because someone in headquarters was uncomfortable with the potential downside of a proposed operation.[11]

The Directorate of Operations has its own unique culture. Part of that culture is the existence of a number of axioms and sayings, which are passed down from generation to generation like tribal lore. Many of them are trite. Most of them are also accurate.

One of the sayings that has been heard increasingly in recent years is as follows: "Big ops, big problems; little ops, little problems; no ops, no problems."

What would Donovan think of that as a mantra?

Let's make it plain and simple: No operation worth doing is without risk. If you go out on the street to conduct an operation, and there is no possible downside, then you are wasting your time on something that is not worth doing. We do not pay the men and women of the CIA to do what is safe and secure; somebody else can do that. We pay them to take risks, to steal what no one thinks can be stolen, to do the impossible.

That said, large organizations respond to broad messages. The bulk of the individuals in any organization are going to do what they are told and what they perceive to be career enhancing. If they see that they are rewarded for taking risks and employing creativity and audacity, they will respond in kind. If they see that those who are most conservative, risk averse, and cautious are promoted and moved up, they will follow that guidance instead.

A number of years ago, a good friend of mine was running an operation focused on the capture of a high-value target who, after staging an attack in which several Americans were killed, had taken refuge in a tribal area among members of his extended family. My friend was successful in locating the target but was hesitant to plan an assault on the area where the target was camping, because of the large number of civilians in the area and the risk of killing or wounding individuals who had no real association with terrorist activity.

Accordingly, with the help of native assets, my friend planned an op to make the extended family members who were providing sanctuary for the target believe that the watering hole they were using for their herd animals had become tainted and unsafe. The plan basically consisted of having an asset leave a dead animal in the watering hole so that it would appear it had died from contamination in the water. This was expected to lead the entire group camped near the watering hole to relocate immediately. Their route out of the immediate area where they were camped could be predicted, and there were numerous locations along the route where it was believed that a capture operation could be carried out successfully and with little risk of collateral damage.

This operation was killed by headquarters on legal grounds. Counsel in Washington DC concluded that we could not guarantee that the animal carcass that would be put in the watering hole would not contaminate the water. Further, counsel decided that if the water were contaminated and if someone did drink the water despite the presence of a dead animal in it we might unintentionally be responsible for illness and even death. This was judged to be an unacceptable level of risk, and the operation was scrubbed.

Keep in mind that the proposal in question was not to throw a dead animal into an otherwise pristine source of water. It was to put a dead animal in a muddy watering hole surrounded by a sea of animal and human waste in a part of the world where you get gastrointestinal problems of almost biblical proportions with breakfast every morning. Nor was the proposal to contaminate the water and not let anyone know about it. The animal carcass would be plainly visible, and there was no question in the minds of the local assets working with us on the op as to what the people camped near the watering hole would do when they saw it. They dealt with this kind of issue every day. They were not idiots—they would decamp in a hurry. Their animals were their lives, and they would not take any chances.

So, having tracked a key target to the ends of the earth and having put together a plan that almost certainly would have delivered the individual in question into our hands without loss of life, my friend was directed to stand down. Ultimately, the target was captured, though not for many more months, and in many other such cases we have not been so lucky.

In the aftermath of September 11, while the entire rest of the United States government spun in circles and a multibillion-dollar defense establishment tried to figure out if it had the ability to strike back, the CIA stepped forward with an immediate plan to go into Afghanistan, destroy the Taliban and al-Qaeda, and kill or capture Osama bin Laden. Fifteen days later CIA officers, under the command of Gary Schroen, were on the ground inside Afghanistan.[12] By late November al-Qaeda and the Taliban were crushed, and the terrorist safe haven in Afghanistan no longer existed. But for the unwillingness of the Bush administration to commit military troops on the ground when repeatedly requested to do so at Tora Bora, Osama bin Laden would also have been killed or captured.

The crushing of al-Qaeda and the Taliban in Afghanistan was by any definition a brilliant success and one that ought to make us take a hard look at other elements of the U.S. government, such as the Pentagon, and examine whether they have the flexibility and creativity required to deal with the threat we are now facing. The men who put together and led the American invasion of Afghanistan and executed it so brilliantly represent what is best in the CIA and our nation.

So where are they now?

We are, as former president George W. Bush said so frequently, in a war against terrorism, an existential conflict that will determine whether we survive as a nation and, perhaps, whether Western civilization survives. The stakes could not be higher. One would be excused, I think, for supposing that we would take the top commanders who were responsible for our greatest victory to date in this war and elevate them to positions from which they could shape our overall strategy and pass on their knowledge and experience to officers under their command.

Gary Schroen had retired prior to September 11. Apparently, the CIA did not believe he had the necessary ability to be retained or that he had what it took to move higher in the ranks. As soon as the towers fell, he was almost immediately recognized as the one guy on the planet most capable of taking in the first team and securing the level of cooperation we needed from the Afghans. He was immediately brought back to active service, and he performed brilliantly. On a shoestring and a prayer, he took in the first team, and he laid the foundation for all the teams that followed.

After his extraction, Gary was once again informed that his services on active duty were no longer required. He returned to retirement. He had filled a need, but that did not change the fact that in the eyes of the organization he did not have what it took to be part of the senior leadership.

Gary Berntsen, mentioned earlier, took command of the Jawbreaker team from Schroen. Under his direction, this team broke the back of Taliban resistance, took Kabul, and hunted bin Laden himself into the mountains at Tora Bora. There, heavily outnumbered and exposed, they took enormous risks to call in air strikes on fleeing al-Qaeda members. Had Army Rangers been deployed to close off the escape routes into Pakistan as Berrntsen and his team requested, they would have brought back bin Laden's head on a platter.

Following the conclusion of his assignment in Afghanistan, Gary Berntsen was replaced as senior officer on the ground by an officer sent in from Washington who had served several key assignments as a staff aide to senior officers in Washington. Berntsen was returned to his Latin American post and retired not long afterward. His willingness to volunteer for the assignment in

Afghanistan did not mark him as having the right stuff for further advancement. If anything, Latin America Division, to which he belonged as a COS in that region of the world, considered it a mark of disloyalty that he had chosen to step up and request reassignment. He is now in private business in New York State.

Cofer Black, the chief of the Counterterrorism Center (CTC), was the individual most responsible for selling President Bush on the bold and unconventional strategy used to seize control of Afghanistan. Known throughout the Directorate of Operations for his aggressiveness and creativity, Cofer was certainly the right man in the right place at the right time for this kind of job. Under his direction a handful of CIA officers working in tandem with U.S. Special Forces (SF) defeated an army of many tens of thousands of men. Following his assignment as chief of CTC, Cofer also went into retirement; he never held another post in the CIA. He is now running a company based in the Washington DC metro area.

The individual at headquarters who really ran the nuts and bolts of the war was Hank Crumpton. He made sure that the teams on the ground had the necessary support, and he directly commanded all the teams other than Jawbreaker. He fought the horrible, bloody bureaucratic wars inside the Beltway to get the men on the ground what they needed. He was brilliant, and his success speaks for itself. Hank also retired not long after the conclusion of the Afghan campaign. He is now working in private industry.

I could go on with this list virtually indefinitely. There are a handful of individuals who commanded elements on the ground during the invasion of Afghanistan who are still on the payroll. None of them is in a key command position. Among them, despite the passage of almost seven years, there is not a single division-level chief. The same could be said of those officers who took the first teams into Iraq. None of them has been moved into a senior-level operational command. Every one of them has either retired or is languishing in some midlevel position, having been passed by in promotion by individuals who kept their heads down, angled for staff jobs, and have never heard a shot fired in anger.

Why? Because they operate within a system that is no longer built to encourage and reward risk taking, daring, and creativity. They operate within a system that keeps "a few Garys" around for those unpleasant times when someone who is not afraid to break the china is required but that is controlled and directed by individuals who will not rock the boat. In times of extreme crisis, the organization may be forced to push such individuals forward to take care of unpleasant tasks, but as soon as the dust begins to settle, it will revert to type, push the "cowboys" aside, and promote individuals who have succumbed to groupthink and display the requisite corporate attitude.

In 1942 a young Italian immigrant to the United States named Max Corvo enlisted in the United States Army. He was dedicated to the struggle against fascism, and he wanted into the fight. After training, he was assigned to the Quartermaster School at Fort Lee, Virginia, where it appeared he was in danger of spending the war filling out forms and performing support tasks.[13]

Corvo was not interested in a safe place to ride out the war. He began to write a plan for organizing intelligence and covert action efforts inside Italy in support of the Allied war effort. His company commander became aware of Corvo's work and sent him off to the base intel section to see if they were interested in Corvo's schemings. They were, and Corvo's plans and thoughts shortly thereafter were circulated outside Fort Lee to a number of other army commands.

One of those commands was the OSS. In short order Corvo, still technically an army private, found himself in a command position within the Italian Section of the OSS. He began to travel widely within the United States, leveraging contacts in the Italian-American community, recruiting personnel for the OSS, and gathering support for its operations. Shortly after the invasion of North Africa by Allied forces, he was dispatched there to begin preparation for OSS operations in support of the impending invasion of Sicily and, ultimately, the Italian mainland.[14]

On arrival in North Africa, Corvo found, not surprisingly, that there was a great deal of work that needed to be done. Virtually no OSS operations were under way, and training facilities for the OSS, provided primarily by the British, were substandard.

There was no existing capability to provide assets going into Italy or other areas occupied by the Axis with alias documentation. There was almost no OSS logistical structure to support the infiltration of personnel. The OSS had no boats on hand; the OSS owned no aircraft. Things were at a complete standstill. The rest of the army was moving ahead, and the OSS in theater was in grave danger of being left behind.

Corvo began a series of meetings with commanders and units across North Africa. He hopped military flights. He bummed rides on transport vehicles. He dispatched individuals under his command—by this time he was a lieutenant—to try to beg, borrow, or steal support for OSS operations. He located an underemployed U.S. Navy PT boat squadron that was itching to get into the war and was staffed with a number of capable, high-energy officers. On his own initiative Corvo conducted a series of meetings with officers in that unit that resulted in their agreement to assist OSS in infiltration operations.

On June 28, 1943, the first team of OSS operatives landed by rubber raft on the island of Sardinia to make contact with partisans and Allied sympathizers and to organize resistance activities. The team launched from a PT boat in the squadron that had been recruited by by Corvo, and Corvo himself was on board that PT boat to ensure that the operation went off as planned. It had been exactly one month to the day from Corvo's arrival in North Africa.[15]

OSS personnel went on to be instrumental in the ultimate seizure of Sardinia, as well as in a host of operations against other Italian islands.[16] By the time the invasion of the Italian mainland was launched, the OSS was capable of deploying a large number of teams by both air and sea in support of Allied offensives. The effort that had been stalled in late May was now running at full speed.

Corvo was, of course, one of many OSS officers who made major contributions to this effort. He was also only one of a very large number of Italian-Americans, many of whom had been born in Italy, who volunteered to undertake hazardous duty in the interest of ridding their homeland of fascism and defending their adopted country, the United States of America. He is identified here less to single him out personally than to illustrate a point.

Corvo was operating within a system that not only encouraged but demanded creativity, audacity, and risk taking. He knew, as did his immediate superior on the ground in North Africa, Colonel Eddy, that what Donovan expected of them was to find a way to get the job done. They understood the risks. They knew that they could and would get men killed, and they understood that in moving quickly they would make mistakes and they would have to modify their plans as they went forward. Some ideas would prove brilliant; some would prove less so. Many lessons would be learned at a horrible expense.

Inaction was, however, not an option. They did not have the luxury of sending messages back to Washington explaining that they were studying various proposals. Standing still would not be tolerated, and reporting that nothing had gone wrong on their watch was not going to be acceptable. Donovan demanded results. He demanded action, and he wanted it now. If they did not or could not produce results, they would be replaced.

Landing a handful of men in a rubber raft launched from a PT boat in 1943 was hardly a risk-free venture. To get to Sardinia the PT boats that carried the team had to travel an extended distance, much of it in broad daylight and within the range of Axis aircraft. The vessels were required to come in close to shore to launch the raft, well within the range of weapons on land, and the likelihood of detection was very high. Once ashore, the team members were forced to make what we would call today "cold contact" with a number of individuals, some of whom might be sympathetic, others of whom might not. The Gestapo was a highly efficient organization, and Axis efforts to infiltrate the ranks of partisans were often very successful. In short, even if the OSS team made it onto Sardinia intact, the possibility that they would be killed or captured once on the island was very high.[17]

The potential rewards were also very high, however, and that brings us back to the central point. If the operation is worth doing, it is going to entail risk. That risk can and should be limited to the maximum extent possible. The risk should be weighed and considered, and a careful balancing of the risk against the prospective gain should be conducted. People's lives are not something to be treated lightly. Losing someone in an operation because no one bothered to take the time to plan the op correctly is not acceptable. Ultimately, though, if we are not prepared to accept that things can and will go wrong, we have no business running operations at all.

Corvo knew all this, and he acted accordingly. Corvo also knew something else, however: He knew that he was not alone in having the attitude he did, and he knew that he was not the only one who felt that action was required. He also knew that those around him not only shared that attitude but were capable by virtue of training and natural ability of doing what had to be done. He was a member of an elite organization, composed of very special people, and he knew that those people were capable of doing extraordinary things and handling extraordinary levels of stress.

That too, unfortunately, has changed. A senior female case officer I know, Maria, with a long history of operational assignments in the Middle East, told me a story once about an experience she had going through paramilitary training shortly after her entrance onto active duty. Maria was going through an exercise in a field environment designed to simulate a survival situation. By the standards of what that often means in a military context, this was a pretty mild exercise, really not much more than the equivalent of a few days of backpacking with some limited instruction on hunting, killing, and cleaning small game, and so on.

At the end of the first day, Maria was in her sleeping bag trying to get some rest. She was stretched out next to another female officer, also in a sleeping bag, and the two had put their shelter halves together to form a small pup tent for shelter. It was late winter, the temperature outside was just above freezing, and there was a mixture of rain and sleet coming down outside. Still, as far as Maria was concerned, she was generally pretty comfortable, both warm and dry, and looking forward to getting a good night's rest.

Then Maria realized the female officer next to her was crying. Maria sat up and asked the other officer what was wrong. The other officer replied that she could not believe that "they" were making her do "this." Maria, genuinely mystified, asked what she was talking about. The other officer replied that she did not believe that it was right that she was expected to sleep outside, on the ground, in the rain. She felt that she was being treated unfairly. She believed that this was not what she had signed up to do.

Somehow, as Maria tells it, she resisted the urge to punch the other officer and eventually got to sleep. She was disgusted, however, and kept wondering to herself as she lay there that night how anyone who could not handle camping out for a few nights was going to handle the danger, stress, and pressure that went with conducting intelligence operations. She made a promise to herself that she would remember the other officer's name and that, if she could help it, she would never work with her once they were out of training. She knew that anyone who would crack under the moderate amount of stress that this exercise had produced had no business being involved in clandestine field work and could not be trusted.

This is not an issue of gender. It is an issue of standards. It is an issue of mind-set.

In northern Iraq during the winter of 2002–2003, a logistics officer assigned to a clandestine CIA team operating with Kurdish intelligence had a seizure behind the wheel of a supply truck. He barely escaped being killed and subsequently had to be evacuated from the country, overland, and moved to CONUS (the continental United States) for treatment. It was determined that the individual in question had epilepsy and had been receiving treatment for his condition for years and that the Office of Medical Services within the CIA was aware of this condition.

Despite this officer's medical condition, he had been cleared for deployment into a highly dangerous environment. The officer had never informed his superiors in northern Iraq or his fellow team members of his condition. No one in OMS had ever passed along this information either. Privacy concerns were deemed to have trumped the operational issues concerned. The first this individual's team leader knew of the medical condition in question was when the crash occurred, and the officer was found to be having a seizure.

The team to which this logistics officer was assigned was operating deep inside northern Iraq against both Iraqi and terrorist targets. All team members were armed, and attempts by both terrorists and Iraqi intelligence to kill CIA personnel on the team were routine. There was no air support for the team; all supplies were brought in overland on bad mountain roads under terrible weather conditions and often at night. The logistics officer with the medical condition was responsible for the bulk of the movement of personnel and supplies in theater and spent large amounts of time behind the wheel of vehicles carrying people and material in areas where a loss of control of a vehicle would likely result in injury or death.

This logistics officer was a former military noncommissioned officer (NCO). He volunteered for this hazardous assignment because he believed in the mission of the CIA, and he wanted to contribute to ridding the world of a brutal dictator. Under very difficult circumstances he did an exceptional job and performed what can only be described as miracles on a routine basis.

That said, almost certainly the logistics officer in question had no business being deployed to the area in question, where medical care was virtually nonexistent, medevac was unavailable, and where stress and fatigue were likely to exacerbate his condition. Without question, also, it was unconscionable to deploy this officer into this environment and not inform the team leader of the medical condition in question. A team operating in this kind of environment is like a single organism. Anything that impacts one officer negatively impacts the whole team. If I cannot function, someone has to take my place. If I cannot walk, someone has to carry me. If I have a seizure behind the wheel of a vehicle on a narrow mountain road in the dead of night, I may very well kill not only myself but everyone else in the vehicle with me.

Yet this was not an aberration. OMS did not respond to this incident by acknowledging that it had erred and promising that it would never happen again. It responded by saying that it had acted in accordance with regulation, that privacy concerns were paramount, and that it would not under any circumstances modify its method of operation in the future.

Several years later in the Middle East, as a chief of station, I had an officer collapse in the middle of the workday and had to get him into a local hospital immediately—he had experienced a brain hemorrhage. We worked round the clock over the next day to get an air ambulance in country and move the stricken individual back to CONUS for treatment. Fortunately, he survived and returned to duty about a year later.

Subsequently, I discovered that this individual had gone through exactly the same thing a few years earlier while assigned to a station in Latin America. I was not told of this in advance, and I had no knowledge of this individual's medical condition nor any way of accessing that information. In the midst of the global war on terrorism, in the heart of the Middle East, I was running operations against brutal, deadly foes, and one of my key personnel, who was routinely deployed into stressful, dangerous situations, was probably by any reasonable standard medically unfit for the duties I was assigning.

I applaud the guts, determination, and courage it took for this individual to return to an overseas posting after one near-death experience. I cannot, however, possibly support a system that allowed it to happen and that concealed all information regarding the condition from the command structure. If an individual goes down in the middle of an op because of a preexisting medical condition, this is not only a threat to that person's safety, it is a threat to everyone else involved in the operation. It means potentially not only that one individual dies unnecessarily but that several other individuals may die as well.

No one in the Office of Medical Services woke up one morning and adopted a policy of concealing medical information on CIA personnel from operational commanders because they wanted to make life just a little bit more difficult in the Directorate of Operations. It wasn't something that was done on a whim or in ignorance either. It was done because in the CIA of today mission accomplishment has taken such a backseat to bureaucratic concerns that personal privacy concerns really have come to trump all other considerations. OMS, operating within the CIA of today, had no choice. They literally had no legal authority to divulge this information.

No one joins Delta Force and seriously believes that he or she has a right to conceal personal medical concerns from a commanding officer. For that matter, people do not enlist in the military, in any service, without fully understanding that they are voluntarily giving up a whole host of personal rights and freedoms in the interest of making the overall force more combat effective. When Max Corvo selected a handful of men out of those available in North Africa and instructed them to undertake a mission that would test them physically and mentally to their utmost, he did not have to wonder if one of them might have epilepsy or think about packing medication for high blood pressure for others. He was functioning as a member of an elite organization. All of his personnel had been screened and rigorously tested. They were prepared to perform under intense pressure and were capable of doing the impossible.

Yet somewhere along the line between 1943 and the present we crossed a line. We began with a common understanding about the kind of individual it took to build a clandestine intelligence organization and the standards that personnel in that organization would have to meet. We have ended up in a place where individuals with serious medical conditions that probably should have disqualified them from overseas service in any capacity can believe that they are as fit as anyone else to participate in dangerous field operations.

The impact of this change in mind-set is felt far beyond the area of medical clearances. Across the board, throughout the length and breadth of the Directorate of Operations, there has been a general erosion of standards for operational personnel, to the point where virtually all personnel have taken to representing themselves as being an "ops officer" regardless of what training they have or have not taken and regardless of their level of overseas experience. It has become a label to be appropriated almost as if one could just begin to call herself a "Marine" because she liked the sound of it, or an Army truck mechanic could decide of his own volition to refer to himself as a "Ranger."

The CIA is composed of a number of different directorates. The core of the organization, however, is the Directorate of Operations (DO). This is the portion of the organization that is focused on the conducting of operations abroad. While crucial support is provided to these operations by individuals assigned to other directorates, it is the men and women of the DO who recruit spies and run clandestine operations.

Within the DO, there are a number of different categories of officers. I would submit, however, that if the DO is the core of the CIA it is case officers who are the core of the DO. Case officers, also known as operations officers, are what the general public means when it talk about "CIA agents." The CIA itself does not use that term. In the CIA an agent is a foreigner who has been recruited by an ops officer to provide intelligence or do other work. The agent is not a staff officer.

Ops officers are the individuals who actually go out and recruit penetrations of terrorist organizations. If you plant a bug in the office of the ambassador of a hostile nation, it is an ops officer who plans the operation, albeit a technical officer who makes it happen. It is also likely an ops officer who recruits the member of the embassy cleaning staff that carries the audio device inside and emplaces it. When a CIA team climbs off a helicopter in a remote tribal area somewhere to set up shop, almost certainly the man or woman in charge of that team is an ops officer.

Trying to describe what makes an ops officer is a difficult task. Training is crucial but probably even more so are innate personal strengths and characteristics. An ops officer has to be able to drink vodka with a Russian SVR (foreign intelligence service) officer until the wee hours of the morning, delving into his contact's soul and exposing great portions of his own in the process, in order to make a key recruitment. He has to be able to smell bullshit in a walk-in's story from a mile away, and he has to be exact in timing, planning, and reporting. He has to be able to work a cocktail party in Hong Kong filled with prominent government officials, and he has to be able to negotiate with a tribal warlord in a remote area of the world. Imagine someone equally good at three-dimensional chess and Texas hold 'em, and you have an idea.

You don't mass-produce people like this. Not just anyone can do the job any more than anyone can be taught to dunk a basketball or write an opera. You have to find people with very special types of skills. You have to subject those people to rigorous training, and then you have to season them through long tours overseas. At the end of that process, you will have ops officers, most of them competent, some of them exceptional. Like making fine wine, it is a process that cannot be hurried.

We seem to have forgotten all of that. A few years ago I was working as a chief of station in the Middle East. A new officer in my shop, who was not an ops officer, wrote up a message on his activities and submitted it to me for transmission. In the message the officer repeatedly referred to himself as a case officer. I bounced the message back to the officer in question, as a teaching point, telling him to edit the message and reminding him that only personnel who are ops certified are to be referred to as case officers.

Minutes later the officer in question showed up in my office. He was offended. He lectured me, protesting that since he was serving overseas in a field capacity he was just as much involved in operations as anyone else. He reminded me, pointedly, of the fact that he had taken some sort of shortened ops-familiarization-type course and that in this course he had actually conducted mock meetings with instructors who were role-playing the part of foreign assets. In his mind there was no functional difference between himself and a case officer who had been fully ops certified and done the job for real down range.

I was in shock. If someone had spit on the floor of a church right in front of me, I could not have felt that a greater sacrilege had been committed. When you have done the job down range for many years and when you know what you and so many others have gone through to produce the intelligence our country so badly needs, it is not a game. There is nothing theoretical about it. You don't become an ops officer by taking a course online. Meeting a role-player for lunch at the Subway restaurant in Crystal City may help give you an appreciation for the basic elements of an ops officer's craft. It does not make you an ops officer any more than my attending a fantasy baseball camp would make me a Major League Baseball player.

The officer in question in this story was thoroughly disabused of his notions as to what did and did not constitute a case officer. He edited his message. He never made the same mistake again, and he went on to have a fine tour. His behavior was not an aberration, however; it was a reflection of a much larger problem.

In the late 1990s I returned to headquarters temporary duty (TDY) from a station in Asia. I was there to discuss a key terrorist case: An officer working under my direction had successfully recruited a member of an extremist group. The case looked good, and we needed to consider our next steps carefully.

I ended up in headquarters, in the bowels of CTC, talking with a roomful of officers who were working the case from the headquarters end. They were excited about the case, but they also had some concerns about the possibility that our asset might be fabricating some of the information he was providing in order to make himself appear more important than he was.

It was a valid concern, one I shared and one we were focused on in station. Anytime you acquire a source that begins to tell you a whole bunch of things you did not know before, there are two very different possibilities. One is that you have acquired a very valuable source and are doing exactly what the CIA is supposed to be doing, telling Washington things no one else knows. The other is that you are being played and all those intel reports you are sending home have about as much basis in reality as Alice in Wonderland.

I told the headquarters officers with whom I was meeting that we were focused on the problem of corroboration and outlined for them what steps we were already taking. I agreed with them that, as in any case, we needed to be sure that we did not get so carried away by the excitement of having recruited an apparently key source that we turned a blind eye to the possibility that our boy just had a creative imagination and was enjoying getting paid for feeding us bullshit.

Then the senior headquarters officer present advised me that he had come up with a plan for testing our source's veracity that he would like implemented. The plan involved placing one of my officers inside this group. I was dumbfounded. For a few moments I struggled to think where to begin in explaining, as diplomatically as possible, that this proposal was one of the dumbest, most frightening things I had ever heard.

Leaving aside the questions regarding our asset and his lack of a track record, who exactly was it that I was going to send undercover to do this job? Working for me at that time were several white women of European descent, several white men of European descent, and one African American male. The women were unusable in this context based on gender. None of the men was Muslim, and none of them was ethnically similar to the individuals against whom we were working.

In response one of the headquarters officers noted that there was an ethnic Arab officer working in the next section who spoke native Arabic. He had a good reputation. He might be available for this job.

I knew the officer in question and had served with him before. He was, in fact, top notch and had done a number of very risky, high-speed ops. I reminded the headquarters officers, however, that none of the persons against whom we were working in this case was of the same ethnicity as this officer. In fact, none of them was an Arab. One Muslim is not the same as any other Muslim. For that matter, in a case like this, it would not be good enough even to have a Muslim officer of the same nationality as the players involved. That would be like thinking that I could penetrate a Ku Klux Klan meeting in Mississippi just because I am white.

And just for a kicker none of this made any difference anyway, because you do not just invite yourself into a clandestine terrorist operation. Terrorists do not take chances, and they do not conduct protracted investigations or legal proceedings. If they suspect you, they kill you, and the only hope you have is that they will make it quick. Our asset could not simply show up for his next contact with the other members of his terrorist cell with a stranger in tow, introduce him as his good buddy Mehmet from the block, and expect that there would be handshakes and greetings all around. Our officer would die. So would our asset.

Despite this, none of my comments seemed to be having any impact. The headquarters officers with whom I was talking were excited about the plan they had come up with—maybe it was based on an episode of *Alias* one of them had seen recently—and they did not want to back off. I, so often accused by my superiors of being overly aggressive, found myself being characterized as "timid."

At some point in this conversation, I stopped and looked around the room, and it sank in that while all of us in the room were speaking English we had no common language. There were at least five headquarters officers present. They represented the key headquarters component responsible for the direction of operations against the Sunni extremist threat worldwide. Not a single one of them was a case officer. Not a single one of them had ever done a permanent change of station (PCS) tour overseas. A couple of them might have done an occasional TDY to Islamabad, picked up a couple of carpets, and hurried home. Other than myself there was not a single person there who had ever met an asset, much less recruited one, or run an op on the street. I was talking about the hard realities of an unforgiving trade; they were talking about something that was to them completely abstract. They were all representing themselves to be "ops officers." Not one of them was.

I am a big believer in the idea that speed and audacity are key in operations. Windows of opportunity open. They also close. To be effective you have to combine speed and audacity with knowledge, experience, and professionalism. If you do that, you have George S. Patton's Third Army going across Europe. If you don't, and all you have left is a desire to take risk without any understanding of what those risks are, then you have George Armstrong Custer at the Little Big Horn. Both men had guts and daring to spare. One cracked the Third Reich. The other led his regiment to slaughter.

An organization is not elite simply because it says it is. This is not a question of labels; it is a question of standards and of professionalism. If you do not maintain those standards and if you do not safeguard that professionalism, the organization decays. The United States Marines are one of the most elite fighting forces on the planet, because they maintain exceptionally high standards, enforce discipline, and refuse to compromise on what is required of their personnel. Imagine a Corps in which physical fitness (PT) tests were no longer administered, rifle training was optional, and boot camp had been reduced to a military familiarization seminar of a few weeks' duration. You might still have individuals wandering around wearing the eagle, globe, and anchor, but you wouldn't have any Marines.

We are, unfortunately, perilously close to this situation in the CIA today. To the extent that the work does get done, and the ops are run, it is a testament to the drive and initiative of individual officers who came to the organization because it was a calling and who do whatever it takes to get the job done. Increasingly, though, they are working within a system that not only does not support them but in many cases actually undercuts them. Why and how we got to this situation will be addressed in the chapters that follow.

CHAPTER TWO

Leadership?

LET'S ASSUME FOR THE SAKE OF ARGUMENT THAT I WANT TO BECOME an officer in the United States Army.[18] Let's also assume, just to simplify the equation, that I choose to pursue this goal by joining the army Reserve Officers' Training Corps (ROTC) at a four-year college somewhere in the United States.

First, I have to secure admission to an ROTC program. This is going to involve an application process, an interview, a medical screening, and so on. Following that relatively simple procedure, however, I am then going to spend the next four years being trained in how to function as an officer. Some of this training will be technical and hands on. I will, for example, learn how to shoot a rifle, throw a hand grenade, and construct a fighting position. Much of it, however, will be focused on how to lead and how to manage.

I will have it drummed into my skull that I will eat last if I eat at all; I will sleep last if I sleep at all. The welfare of my personnel comes first; it is my responsibility to take care of them. They will not follow me into combat just because I have gold bars on my collar and tell them to. They will follow me because they respect and trust me.

I will learn that the success and failure of my unit is my responsibility and my responsibility alone. If the unit does not pass an inspection, it will not be acceptable for me to blame my personnel. They work for me, and I am in command. It is my job to ensure that the unit accomplishes its mission, but if the unit fails, it is my obligation and duty to accept responsibility for that failure.

By the same token if the unit succeeds it is not acceptable for me to take credit for that achievement and bask in the limelight. I did not do the bulk of the work; my people did. They deserve the credit. Shoulder the blame. Pass along the praise.

And throughout this long four-year process, which includes both copious amounts of classroom work and long periods of field exercises and training, I will be evaluated. My acceptance as an army officer is not a foregone conclusion. If I do not demonstrate that I have what it takes to lead in a combat situation, I will be asked to leave. If I do not show that I can learn from experience and avoid repeating the same errors, I will be told that my services are not required.

At the conclusion of this four-year period, if I have performed satisfactorily, I will be commissioned as a second lieutenant in the United States Army. Then the real work will begin.

First, I will go to a basic officers' training course of some kind. Exactly which one of these I attend will be dependent on my branch assignment. If I am, for example, an Armor officer, I will go to Fort Knox, Kentucky, and will spend roughly the next four months in intensive training in preparation for my first actual unit assignment. During these four months I will receive a lot of instruction in the operation of weapons systems, the tactical employment of men under my command, and other technical subjects. I will also continue to receive heavy doses of instruction on leadership and management. I will rotate through student command positions, where my ability and understanding will be tested and evaluated. If I do not measure up, I will be recycled to repeat the training or I will be sent home.

Assuming I successfully complete my basic officers' training course, and assuming I do not go on to additional training, such as jump school, I will then, finally, report to my first unit. I will be introduced to my platoon sergeant, who technically works for me but probably has fifteen years on active duty. I will be reminded that I know exactly nothing and told to spend the bulk of my time in my first few months learning from my platoon sergeant and working hard to become a little less ignorant.

Looking over my shoulder the entire time will be the company executive officer and the first sergeant. They will ensure that no mistake made by me goes unnoticed. They will ride me. They will prod me. They will make me a better officer.

Above them will be my company commander. On those occasions when my ego gets the better of me and I start to think I am the reincarnation of George S. Patton or I make excuses for failure, the company commander will put the fear of God into me. I will learn, the hard way, to put the lessons I have been taught into practice. I will stay late with my men in the motor pool when they are working long hours to repair deadlined vehicles. I will spring for the beer and burgers at impromptu platoon picnics designed to raise morale. I will ask my wife, out of the goodness of her heart, to visit the wives of men in my unit and check on them while the unit is out on extended field exercises.

At the conclusion of several years of this, if I have worked hard and listened, I will actually know what I am doing. I will be a leader, and I will be ready to move on and become a company commander myself.

The army, however, will ensure that if I remain on active duty I will be continuously trained and guided in how to improve my leadership ability and how to manage ever larger and more complex organizations. Before I become a company commander, for example, I will have to attend another advanced officer training course of several months' duration. Throughout my career I will be cycled through other schools designed to prepare me for my next level of command. Much of the training I receive will be technical or organizational. Throughout it all, however, will be the constant drumbeat of the standards to which a leader is held. As I rise in rank, I will realize that with every promotion the bar is set just a little bit higher. By the time I am a field grade officer, I will understand that the eagles on my shoulder do not mean I get a free ride. They mean I have no excuse for failure.

Let's contrast this system and approach with the CIA's methodology for selecting, training, and cultivating leaders: There is none.

The DO is the heart of the CIA, and case officers are the heart of the DO. They are the equivalent of infantry officers in the U.S. Army. There are thousands of other individuals who make critical contributions to the mission of the DO, but it is case officers who recruit spies and produce intelligence. It is also case officers who run both the DO and the CIA. Below the level of the director, who is usually a political appointee, it is case officers who hold the key senior command positions.

Case officers are recruited through an elaborate and highly refined process.[19] Whether it could be improved is a topic for another time and place. For our purposes here, let it suffice to say that the CIA has been recruiting case officers for a long time and, generally speaking, has a pretty good handle on what kind of personality traits lend themselves to the profession. The CIA does, overall, a good job of finding and hiring officers who will do an effective job of running operations and recruiting spies. Nothing in this recruitment process, however, is focused on the identification of individuals with leadership or managerial ability.

Once recruited and through training, a case officer will generally be posted to a station. There, he or she will run ops and recruit sources; most of this will be done as a singleton. Increasingly, in today's counterterrorist work a case officer may have to work as part of a team with other officers, but even then the case officer will be performing as an individual, not as a leader or a manager.

Assuming that the case officer does a good job, he or she will be promoted. Such promotion will be based on how many sources the officer has recruited, how many intel reports these sources have produced, and similar criteria. These promotions will not be based on any measure of leadership ability or potential.

Within several years, assuming the case officer in question is doing well, he or she will likely be moved into a management position of some kind. This may be a midlevel position in a station overseas. It may even be an independent command as a base chief or chief of a small station.

In preparation for this move into management ranks, the case officer will receive no training of any kind other than, perhaps, a short seminar of some type. There will be no selection process. If the case officer has done a good job recruiting and running ops, he will be judged capable of managing, leading, inspiring, and motivating. The fact that *there is no earthly reason to assume any linkage whatsoever between competence in individual skills and the ability to command will not be considered.*

Once in a managerial capacity, the case officer's further progress will be measured largely by how well he or she does in furthering the corporate interests of the organization. As addressed at some length earlier, these are increasingly defined as avoiding failure. A case officer will not function in a system that demands achievement but will function instead in a system that considers that if nothing goes wrong on his watch he has done a good job. Not insignificantly, he will work for individuals who have been "selected" by the same system. Knowing nothing about how to lead or manage himself, he will work for senior officers who are equally ignorant.

What results will be a self-perpetuating caste of individuals who may, at least, have a decent grasp of the fundamentals of clandestine intelligence operations but who know nothing of leadership or management. Being atrocious leaders themselves, they will not only perform poorly in positions of authority but naturally will be resistant to any suggestion that they could improve their level of performance or carry out their duties in a more efficient or even more just fashion. When attacked or criticized, they will circle the wagons, reject all criticism, and, whenever possible, they will promote into the inner circle only those individuals who are equally as ignorant of the facets of leadership and management as they are. Starry-eyed dreamers talking reform and change will be shoved aside. "Yes men" who pose no threat will be pushed along.

Imagine if the United States Army utilized the same "system."

In place of the current elaborate structure, the United States Army could have a process by which a series of tests would be administered to the members of each platoon. Then that enlisted man with the best PT scores, the top marks at the rifle range, and the most highly shined boots would be chosen to be the platoon leader and promoted to second lieutenant. His boss, the company commander, would be the guy who won the competition a few years earlier.

Would it really be a great surprise to anyone if this system failed to produce particularly gifted leaders and managers? Would it really shock anyone if the company commander and his newly minted platoon leader were to defend this "system" and resist any attempt to modify promotion criteria and focus on leadership capacity at the expense of PT scores?

No one with any degree of common sense would expect that the size of a guy's biceps and his proficiency with a firearm would necessarily be any kind of indication of his ability to organize complex undertakings or to inspire his fellow soldiers. Whatever correlation was found to exist would be purely coincidental. One set of skills and abilities has nothing to do with the other.

A platoon leader in the army needs to be in good shape. He must be able to keep up with his troops, and he needs to set a good example. Whether he is or is not the best athlete is irrelevant. It is not his job to be the first man over the wall into a target compound or to set a world record in doing so. It is his job to decide whether or not the wall needs to be scaled and to come up with a good plan for taking down the compound. To the extent he needs to demonstrate that he too can climb the wall, it is less about tactical necessity and more about showing that he will subject himself to the same dangers that his men face.

The same applies to the platoon leader's ability to handle his weapon: He must be able to perform in combat. He needs to be able to show his troops that he is not asking them to do anything he cannot do himself. His primary function, however, is not to serve as a rifleman. His job is to organize, to lead, to inspire, to direct. Major Dick Winters, famous from his prominent mention in the book *Band of Brothers,* never again fired his weapon in combat after the invasion of Normandy. His unit served on the front for the remainder of the war and participated in such actions as the Battle of the Bulge. Winters was crucial to the unit's success in all those engagements, but it was not his role as a rifleman that made his participation significant—it was his role as a leader.

Similarly, a CIA officer running operations and managing other officers needs to know the business. He needs to have demonstrated that he can recruit and that he can run secure ops. Whether he is the top recruiter in station, though, is irrelevant. If he is going to serve in a command capacity, what is crucial is that he can lead and that he can manage.

In the CIA today there are a number of officers who have done exceptionally well as individual case officers, have been promoted, and have shown themselves to be gifted leaders as well. I would submit, however, that when this happens under the current system it is pure luck. Some of the agency's senior officers also turn out to be gifted artists and skilled musicians. That does not mean there is anything about the current way of business that assists in identifying these individuals as good leaders.

Many, many more of the individuals who are elevated to command positions have very limited leadership and management ability. They were chosen for their individual skills, and they were promoted based on those skills. No one ever tested them to see if they could lead or manage, and no matter what level of such ability they might have had, no one ever gave them any training to cultivate it.

This does not mean necessarily that they are bad officers. They were not recruited or trained to run large organizations or to lead; they were recruited for their ability to function as individual case officers. It is, ultimately, not their fault that they have been pushed into management and leadership positions for which they are ill suited. It is the fault of the organization, which sixty years after its founding has never developed any system for the selection, training, and cultivation of leaders.

Within the CIA there is, in fact, no real alternative mechanism for the recognition of individual accomplishment other than promotion of the individual in question into a leadership position. If I recruit several penetrations of Russian intelligence in one tour, I am going to get promoted. If I continue this level of achievement, I am going to get promoted again. In short order this record of accomplishment is going to put me into some kind of leadership position, and it may even mean that I become a chief of station somewhere relatively quickly.

As a chief of station, it will be my job to mentor the junior officers under my command and to plan and direct operations.

It will be my job to handle the budget, manage the infrastructure, plan ahead for emergencies, counsel difficult personnel, and, above all else, motivate and inspire my troops. An exceptional chief of station for whom I once worked described a large portion of his job as being a "cheerleader." Being a case officer is difficult, dangerous, frustrating work. It is lonely. Without encouragement and guidance, many promising young officers will fail.

What is it in my background, experience, or training as a CIA officer that will prepare me to handle these challenges? As noted already, nothing. One day my job is to recruit spies and push intel back to Washington. The next day I am sitting in my office balancing the books, figuring out how to deal with an ambassador who is hostile to the CIA's mission in country, and counseling a female officer who just found out that her husband, also an employee in station, is having an affair. If I flounder, it will be no great surprise.

The personality of many case officers is yet another complicating factor. Case officers come in all sizes, shapes, and categories. They all do their work, which is more art than science, in their own particular way. Some find common ground with targets in strip joints and smoky back rooms. Others are more likely to bond with individuals with a fine taste in history and wine.

Some of these individuals are gregarious and naturally outgoing. I served in Asia once with a former college quarterback. Another officer with whom I worked in the Mediterranean was an accomplished actor. A significant number of effective case officers, however, are going to fall into the category of individuals probably best described as "forced" extroverts. They are not naturally outgoing or comfortable in large groups. They are by instinct loners, introspective and uncomfortable with opening up or exposing their true feelings. It may, in fact, be something about this combination of personality traits that forces them to become more calculating and premeditated in their dealings with other people. They have learned from childhood to think through carefully their interactions with the rest of humanity.

For an individual trying to work his way into the soul of a terrorist considering betraying his comrades, these kinds of personality traits may be very valuable. It pays to be able to read the lines on someone's face, to know what it means when he or she avoids eye contact, to sense the significance not only in what is said, but, even more so, in what is not said. It can be a great advantage to have the capacity to dispassionately manage and manipulate all your personal interactions in such a way as to further a personal aim. If you are naturally uncomfortable with others and have had to learn to put on a false face for the world throughout your life, you may find that you are well suited for the sort of "double existence" espionage often requires.

Such characteristics are not nearly as desirable in an officer who is charged with inspiring, motivating, guiding, and directing. They may, in fact, prove to be the kiss of death and render this individual completely incapable of doing what is required of him as a leader. A leader cannot "act a part." He has to live it; he has to be genuine.

Late in the Second World War, William Colby, a future director of Central Intelligence, led a mission into Nazi-occupied Norway. The goal of the operation was to sever the Nordland rail line and to prevent upwards of 150,000 German troops from redeploying out of Norway. As conceived, it required Colby and twenty OSS operatives to jump into Norway, proceed overland by cross-country ski, and attack the rail line, which was at the bottom of sheer cliffs several hundred feet tall.[20]

The team went in via three aircraft, seven men to a plane. One aircraft mistakenly dropped its personnel in Sweden, where they were detained. The fourteen remaining men made it safely to the ground and married up with assets already in place inside Norway. Efforts to send reinforcements from England were frustrated when two separate aircraft crashed and ten OSS personnel were killed.

Colby, already missing one third of his force, pushed on. The weather was horrific. The team was lashed by high winds, sleet, and snow, and skiing was almost impossible. The first day they made fifteen miles; the second day it was twenty-five. Only by almost superhuman exertion did they make their destination.

Upon arrival at the site, Colby discovered that the ice storm that had made movement so difficult for him and his team had coated the cliffs overlooking the rail line with inches of ice.

Descent seemed impossible, and he was advised by the experienced ski personnel on his team that there was no way they could find a way down safely under these conditions.

Colby refused to quit. Members of his team located a frozen waterfall proceeding down the cliff face in stages through a gorge. The team, sliding and slipping, improvised a method to descend. At the rail line they emplaced their charges and destroyed the target bridge. Then, evading German troops the entire distance, they proceeded overland to a base camp on the Swedish border and safety.

It reads like something out of any one of a thousand war movies we have all seen. It is not fiction, however; it is fact. More to the point, it is representative of hundreds of such operations carried out by OSS across the face of the globe. Colby's performance was superb, but he was serving in very good company.

In late 1943 Lieutenant Alexander "Alekko" Georgiades was an OSS officer serving undercover as a diplomat in the Greek consulate in the Turkish city of Edirne. Edirne is situated near the border between Greece and Turkey. and over a period of many months, Georgiades made three dozen trips into Greece to meet with Greek partisans and to lay the groundwork for attacks on key railroad bridges over which critical shipments of chromium were brought from Turkey into German-controlled territory. This supply of chromium was vital to German war efforts, and stopping it would be of immense value to the allies.[21] Inside occupied Greece, as Georgiades met with the partisans, his cover status as a Greek diplomat was of no value to him whatsoever. If caught by the Germans, he was not going to be expelled; he was going to be brutalized, then executed.

By April 1944 Georgiades had secured the necessary agreement from key partisan leaders to allow the operation to proceed. He helped OSS captain James Kellis and two radiomen, Spyridon Kapponis and Michael Angelos, to infiltrate into Greece from Turkey across the Evros River. After a difficult trek through mountainous terrain, the team was successful in meeting up with the Greek guerrillas and began the lengthy, often frustrating task of organizing an assault force and fine-tuning planning for attacking the bridges. At one point during this process, Kellis, Angelos, and a team of guerrillas were surrounded and attacked by a German force. They escaped only after a seven-hour gun battle. Three of the Greek members of the group were severely wounded.

Airdrops of equipment and supplies were brought in via OSS-controlled aircraft. Another OSS officer, Lieutenant Everette Athens, piloted an OSS caique, essentially a converted Greek fishing boat, through waters patrolled by German vessels from Turkey to deliver three additional team members and more equipment.

On May 27, 1944, after several days of infiltration through areas dotted with German guard posts, Kellis, Athens, and 170 Greek partisans arrived in the vicinity of their targets. Over the next two days, as they observed the security forces in the area and finalized planning, the team counted nine freight trains consisting of 283 rail cars of war supplies cross the largest of the spans, the 210-foot-long Svelingrad bridge.[22]

The attack on the Svelingrad bridge began at 11:00 p.m. on May 29, 1944. Shortly after the charges had been placed on the bridge supports, the German guards became aware that something was amiss and began firing. It was too late. The bridge was completely demolished in the ensuing explosion.

Kellis, Athens, and their team then began a forced march, pursued all the while by an entire battalion of German troops. They successfully eluded the Germans, and during the trek Greek partisan members of the team organized an ambush of the pursuers that resulted in the death of the German battalion commander and his staff.

Meanwhile, a second OSS team, operating under the direction of Angelos, approached a smaller bridge guarded by Greek gendarmes. Angelos, speaking in native Greek, persuaded the guards not to offer resistance. After they had moved the guards safely out of harm's way, the team then proceeded to destroy this structure as well.[23] The result of these twin attacks was a major disruption of the flow of chromium into the Third Reich.

People who have heard shots fired in anger and put their lives on the line know that people do not follow you in the kind of circumstances described above just because you tell them to. They don't do it because you yell, stomp your foot, or threaten to write something adverse in their next fitness report either. When you are deep inside hostile territory, battered by severe weather and faced with the very real prospect of imminent death, you follow the man or woman who commands your respect.

Respect is earned. It doesn't come with the bars you pin on your collar or with your last GS promotion. If you lead by example, if you care for your people, if you stand up for them when they need you, if you prove to them that they can trust you and believe in you, respect will follow. If you don't, God help you—you are lost.

In the 1990s I was serving in a station in Asia as a midlevel manager. I supervised a number of more junior officers and reported to the COS, who was a very senior officer with roughly twenty-five years of service.

One day we got a report from an asset that suggested a particular operation might be compromised. Even more damaging, depending on exactly how the information was interpreted and how much of it you believed, it raised the possibility that many other operations had been compromised as well. Maybe it was nothing, but then again, maybe it meant we were faced with a massive debacle.

I reported the information immediately to the COS. He was obviously very concerned and directed me to call a meeting of all operational personnel immediately. I did so. We assembled in a conference room within minutes and awaited the COS's arrival.

Moments later the COS walked in the door and sat down. Without any preliminary discussion he advised us that he had reviewed the information we had just acquired and there was no doubt in his mind that the very worst had happened. We were compromised across the board. It was a disaster.

The COS then went on to say that he had foreseen this debacle coming for many months and that he had tried on many occasions to warn us. (I did not then and I do not now have any idea what he meant by this.) He noted that we had decided to ignore him, and therefore, this disaster was our doing and our problem. He suggested that we needed to put our heads together and come up with a plan fast. He told us he hoped we had learned from this event and that in the future we would pay attention to him.

Then the COS left the room, went back to his office, and shut the door.

If you had dropped a hand grenade in the conference room, you could not have produced a more dramatic effect. The entire group present was literally speechless.

Visualize a sailing vessel at sea in the midst of a raging storm. Waves are breaking over the bow. Surf is crashing on nearby rocks. The rudder is not answering the helm. Lightning is crackling in the sky. The terrified crew turns to the captain and awaits his orders.

And the captain advises that he knew the storm was coming, but no one would listen to him, so now it is the crew's problem to figure out what to do. He disappears below decks. The crew is left to face the tempest alone.

We shuffled out of the conference room. I went back to my office and sat, stunned, at my desk. I grew up in a military family; principles of leadership were ingrained in every element of my upbringing. I could not conceive of a situation in which an officer in command would abdicate his responsibility and choose to act like a petulant little child instead of a leader.

The other more junior officers filtered in and took seats in my office as well. Some of them started to bitch about the COS and denigrate him. I told them to shut up. No matter what I felt, I was still working for the chief, and it was my responsibility to be a loyal subordinate and not undercut his authority.

Someone asked the inevitable question: What do we do now?

I hesitated. Then I did the only thing I could do: I made a decision. I told the officers assembled to ignore the COS's comments. I told them I disagreed with his analysis, that I did not believe any of our operations had been compromised. I instructed them to hold course until and unless we acquired other information that would suggest I was wrong. Then we mapped out a plan to test all our sources for possible counter-intelligence issues and assigned responsibility for getting a full report on the whole situation written up and cabled back to headquarters immediately.

Thankfully, time proved my analysis was correct. We did not have a problem. We weathered the storm; life went on much as before, and we continued to provide timely, valuable intelligence. The COS never once made any subsequent reference to his comments in the conference room, and after a few days of keeping a low profile, he reemerged and acted as if nothing had happened. In station we followed his lead and continued on as we had before.

We had learned, however. We had learned that when the chips were down and a leader was most required, we could not count on the COS. Not only would he not make a decision, but he would immediately sacrifice all of us and blame any problems on our "incompetence." "Shoulder the blame and pass along the praise" had morphed. It was now "In a crisis begin by designating a scapegoat."

There are, I think, two key points that must be emphasized in connection with the story related above. First, no matter how repulsive I found the COS's actions in this situation, ultimately, I know it was not his fault. The blame properly rests with the organization and the system that put a man like this COS into a senior leadership position in a field environment.

This COS was one of the most intelligent officers with whom I ever served. He was exceptionally well read and well spoken. He had immense knowledge of history and of the craft of intelligence. He was an expert on Soviet intelligence organizations, their methodologies, and the key personalities within them. If you wanted a man to sit surrounded by stacks of files and myriad computer screens and to swim through the maze of mirrors that counterintelligence work often becomes, he was perfect for the job. The chief's ability to retain and process mountains of minute details and synthesize them into a coherent whole was incredible.

But the chief was not a leader. It was not just that the COS was a bad leader—he was devoid of any understanding of what the role of a leader was and incapable of even attempting to fulfill it. He did not walk into the conference room that day and do a bad job of leading. He walked into the conference room that day without even a faint understanding of what was required of him. He had signed up to run operations, and he apparently did it well. At no point as he was promoted and moved up the ladder did anyone ever say to him that his job had changed or suggest to him that he was now expected to fulfill a fundamentally different set of requirements. A leader would have walked into the conference room that day conscious of the magnitude of the threat facing station operations and recognized that his first job was to inspire confidence and let the troops know that he was in charge and everything was going to be okay. If you had laid that out for the COS in question, he would have had no idea what you were talking about.

The second key point that I think needs to be made is that this incident was not an aberration. Any large organization has good officers and bad. Anyone who has worked in a large organization has horror stories of incompetent managers and leaders. You cannot build a unit of any size and delude yourself that all of your personnel will always be top notch. The world does not work like that. That said, the behavior of the COS I have described above is unfortunately representative of much of agency senior leadership today.

Early in my career I was involved in an operation against a terrorist target that went horribly wrong on the street. The details of that incident cannot be discussed in an unclassified context—suffice to say that a number of gross tradecraft errors were made by officers involved, and a debacle ensued. I came very close to getting killed, as did a number of other officers. I spent several very, very long minutes with the barrel of a loaded weapon jammed against the base of my skull while I was doing my best to talk my way out of a dire predicament.

Once the gun had been removed from my head, I was taken into custody and subjected to some fairly extensive questioning. It was a long way from interrogation by the Gestapo, but it wasn't the best time I've ever had either. Held with me was another officer, grabbed during the same operation.

While we were still being held, my COS was alerted to the unfolding debacle and summoned into the office. Other officers, who had arrived in station ahead of him, briefed him on what had occurred and gave him the best information they could provide as to where the other officer and I were being held.

My COS had his priorities straight. Prior to taking any action to confirm our location or secure our release, he pulled up all message traffic regarding the operation in the computer database and then began to delete any such messages that had not yet been released and transmitted to headquarters. His motive in doing so was to eliminate as much of the record as he could regarding the details of how the operation had been planned and conducted to give himself the maximum capacity to protect his own equities and shift responsibility to his subordinates. In short, before he even knew for sure whether we were still alive, he began working on covering his ass.

When I was going through training as a young lieutenant, one of the things on which we focused a great deal of time and effort was mounted land navigation. We would pile several young officers into an armored personnel carrier (APC) under the direction of an NCO instructor and spend the day perfecting our capacity to move our personnel and vehicles quickly and effectively from point A to point B under a variety of field conditions in daylight and during hours of darkness.

One day we were out doing this kind of exercise, and we happened to have the great good fortune of drawing Sergeant First Class Champion as an instructor. SFC Champion was a superb NCO. He was also no nonsense. He knew exactly what he wanted in a platoon leader when he was serving as a platoon sergeant, and he had no intention whatsoever of accepting anything less than that from us as trainees.

A group of us, all young lieutenants, were seated inside an APC waiting to begin training. Champion climbed in, shoved a map into the hands of the lieutenant closest to him, and told him to move immediately to an alternate location, designated by a set of ten-digit grid coordinates. Champion spat out these coordinates in rapid-fire fashion. He did not repeat them.

The lieutenant who had been handed the map looked lost. He looked down at the map and then back at Champion. He began to ask a series of confused, fumbling questions.

Champion grabbed the map back. He told the lieutenant he was "dead" for the remainder of the exercise. Then Champion handed the map to the next lieutenant and repeated his instructions.

This lieutenant did not make the same mistake as the first officer. He said nothing. He hunched over the map, scribbled down the coordinates Champion had given on a piece of paper in a notebook, and then began to map out a route to the new position.

A few moments passed. The lieutenant continued to study his map and plan his route. Then Champion grabbed the map away from him, told this officer he also was "dead," and handed the map to me. He did not repeat the coordinates or his instructions.

I am not necessarily the brightest child. When working on the property back home, my father used to refer to me as a "strong back and a weak mind." That doesn't mean I am an idiot. I had seen what transpired, and I had learned.

I had no idea what exact route we needed to take to get where Champion wanted us to go. I did know, however, from the coordinates given that we were headed north of where we were and that to get anywhere we were going to have to climb down and off the hill on which we were sitting and make it to a dirt road nearby. So before I looked at the map, and while I was still climbing up into the vehicle commander's seat, I told the driver to move out and to take us downhill, onto the road, and head north. Then, once I made it to the commander's seat, I laid out the map on the top of the APC and fine-tuned our route.

Champion did not "kill" me.

Anybody who has ever gone through military training probably has a dozen similar stories. The point is obvious and clear: If you are in command, command. Make a decision. Take responsibility. Do not hesitate. Do not dither. Do not seek to transfer the weight of your position onto others. If you do not want to make the calls and take the hits, you have no business being in a leadership position in the first place.

For our purposes here, though, there is another, larger point on which we need to focus. Champion did not get into the APC that day and, all on his own, just because he was feeling adventurous, decide to enforce a set of standards that he thought might be of value. He got into the APC and taught us the same way he had taught hundreds of other officers and NCOs before us and the same way he himself had been taught.

It never occurred to us to push back against Champion, to argue with him, or to dispute his interpretation of these standards.

However much difficulty we were having with satisfying the expectations of our instructors, we knew what those expectations were. We shared the same values. We believed in the same things. We had joined the army to be leaders, and at least intellectually, we understood what that meant.

A Marine lieutenant whose unit has failed inspection and is required to stay late in the barracks and remedy its deficiencies does not tell his troops that it is their problem and go home to his quarters to watch television. He knows that, first and foremost, if the unit has failed, it is a reflection on him and his leadership. Not only does he stay—he is the last man out at the end of the day. He sets the standard. He leads by example, and he makes no excuses.

He does not do this, however, purely because of some internal drive. He does it because that is what is required of him by the system in which he functions. His fellow officers all live by the same creed. The man or woman who leads from the front, who sets the bar, who takes the blame when things go wrong and passes the credit on to his or her troops when things go well is not an aberration. This is the rule, not the exception, and the entire Marine Corps from the ground up is structured in such a way as to ensure that this remains the case.

There is no such system in place within the CIA, and the long-term effect is catastrophically corrosive.

During the time I was in Iraq, I had the privilege of having as a deputy one of the finest officers with whom I ever served. He led the first CIA team into the city of Mosul in the spring of 2003. He won the Intelligence Star, came under fire personally on numerous occasions, broke the back of the Iraqi Fifth Corps in his area of operations, crushed the resistance of the Fedayeen and Muhabarat, and enjoyed the immense respect of the men and women under his command. Had he received the cooperation of the U.S. military commander in his area he very likely would have delivered the surrender of most of the Iraqi forces in the north and quite possibly have changed the entire course of postoccupation events.

At the conclusion of his tour of duty, he was returned to the same post in which he had been serving before he volunteered to go into combat and put to work under a former subordinate. The fact that this subordinate was also a superb officer did not take away the sting. My deputy's reward for having lived up to the highest possible standards that could be expected of a leader, spent a year away from his family, and risked his life on numerous occasions was—exactly—nothing.

During this same time frame, while out of Iraq in headquarters for a series of meetings, I encountered an old classmate of mine in the halls and asked him what he was up to. He made a series of highly disparaging comments about the "war on terror" and the invasion of Iraq and noted to me that he "did not join up to kill people." He had been approached about taking a job in Afghanistan and had refused; he was not interested in taking a hardship tour that would require him to spend time away from his family. He had instead gotten himself a job working in the front office of the division to which he was assigned as the equivalent of a staff aide. A year later, having leveraged his access to the front office, he secured himself a position as COS in a major European post. His punishment for having shirked his responsibilities, hidden from danger, and allowed others to shoulder his share of the load was—exactly—nothing.

Every major internal study of the CIA done in the last five years of which I am aware has pointed to the lack of quality senior leadership as the single biggest threat to the future of the organization. It is, without question, the reason most experienced officers depart. Studying is one thing, however, and taking action is another. As long as the reports that talk about problems with leadership are being handed to the very same leaders who are the problem, it is hard to see how any real change is going to occur.

Fundamentally, no change is ever made. From time to time long messages are sent to the field regarding the need for "leadership," Requirements are periodically imposed that new managers must attend "seminars" or "off sites," at which they will learn to parrot buzzwords and to feign interest in the welfare of their subordinates and self-sacrifice. Then they return to their offices and proceed to behave precisely as they did the day before. This is not a system for selecting and training leaders; it is a "check the box" exercise designed to give the impression of change without actually threatening the status quo in any real fashion. One suspects that this is what The Who had in mind: "Smile and grin at the change all around/Pick up my guitar and play/Just like yesterday."

When all is said and done, though, the lack of leadership in the CIA, while a huge problem, is still only one piece of a very complex puzzle. The CIA, so desperately needed at this juncture in our nation's history, is suffering from a host of other crippling ailments as well. It is the deadly combination of all these factors that has mortally wounded this increasingly vital agency.

CHAPTER THREE

Calcification

Arguably the single most effective OSS operative inside occupied France during the Second World War was a one-legged American woman named Virginia Hall.[24] Hall was born in 1906 in Baltimore, Maryland, into a prominent family. Her life as the daughter of a successful businessman was secure, and she was expected to lead a life befitting her status, marry well, and focus on her duties as mother and wife.

Hall had other ideas. She was an avid movie buff and from a young age had taken a keen interest in international relations and foreign cultures. She attended Radcliffe and Barnard Colleges, pursued studies in foreign languages (French, Italian, and German), and in 1931 secured a clerical position working in the Department of State. When she joined State, she left her secure stateside existence behind for good.

The first position in which Hall served overseas was as a clerk in the American Embassy in Warsaw, Poland. She went on over the next few years to hold positions in Tallinn, Vienna, and Izmir, where she was accidentally injured. While hunting, she dropped her shotgun, and as she attempted to regain control of the weapon, it discharged, striking her in the foot. Gangrene set in before she could be rushed to a hospital, and part of her left leg below the knee was amputated to save her life.

Hall was fitted with a wooden leg, which she nicknamed "Cuthbert," and which became the basis of one of the many noms de guerre by which she was later known. Her comrades in the French Resistance during World War II referred to her as *la dame qui boite,* or “limping lady.”[25] This was also the name by which she was known to the Gestapo, which hunted her relentlessly.

The accident meant the end of Hall's career in the State Department. There was a firm regulatory policy against the retention of any employee who had suffered the amputation of any portion of any limb, and Hall was forced to resign. It was May 1939. When World War II began later that same year, Hall was living in Paris. She immediately responded to the initiation of hostilities by enlisting in the French Ambulance Corps as a Private Second Class.

When France fell in June 1940, Hall fled to England. She secured a position as a clerk in the office of the military attaché in the U.S. embassy in London, and while in that position, she was recruited by the British Special Operations Executive (SOE) to go back into France undercover and to report intelligence on German activities there.

SOE was created by the British government in July of 1940 to undertake sabotage and covert action inside German-occupied Europe. It was to gather intelligence as well, but from the outset it was designed to wage war. In the words of Winston Churchill, he wanted it to “set Europe ablaze.”[26]

As a new recruit Hall received the usual training in weapons, communications, and other skills. She was then sent back inside occupied France to set up resistance networks in what was now Vichy, France. Her cover was as a reporter for the *New York Post.*

Hall first worked out of Vichy, France, and then in early 1942 relocated to Lyon. She made contact with resistance leaders, facilitated the return of downed airmen and escaped prisoners to England, and reported on the situation inside occupied France. When America entered the war, Hall officially became an enemy alien and had to take her entire operation underground to avoid capture by the Germans and by Vichy forces.

In November 1942 the Germans directly occupied Vichy, France. A flood of German troops entered the country, and Hall was forced to flee over the Pyrenees Mountains in the dead of winter on foot. She was detained briefly in Spain and then, with the assistance of the U.S. consul, released. She immediately resumed her career as an intelligence officer.

Hall operated briefly in Madrid and then returned to England. She received training as a radio operator and then was transferred out of SOE into the fledgling OSS. She received the code name "Diane," and at her request she was sent back inside France.

Inside France Hall organized resistance activities and collected intelligence on German troop dispositions and plans. She was hunted continuously by the Gestapo and was forced to change residences and hide sites almost daily. She refused to be deterred, going out frequently into the street herself, dressed as a peasant woman, to collect key intelligence directly. Teams under her direction attacked trains, downed telephone lines, blew up bridges, and, as the Germans retreated following the Normandy invasion, captured over five hundred enemy troops themselves. As the result of her actions, the Gestapo assessed her to be the most dangerous Allied agent in all of Europe.

After the war, Hall was given the Distinguished Service Cross for her actions. General Donovan requested that the president himself give the award to Hall because of the magnitude of her accomplishments. Hall refused the honor, saying she had work to do and that such a public display was inconsistent with her status as an active operator. Instead, the award was given to her quietly by General Donovan himself.[27]

I have taken the time to acknowledge Virginia Hall's service at some length for a variety of reasons. First, certainly, because she did her nation a great service and deserves to be remembered. There is an exhibit in her honor in the CIA Museum at Langley. More serving officers should take the time to stop in and see it.

I think Hall's story is important also, however, because of what it tells us about the way the OSS approached its mission and the simple, elegant, even brutal methodology it employed. It is, I think, critical that we think about it if we are serious in wanting to improve the functioning of our current intelligence apparatus.

In 1944 we were at war. We were engaged in a death struggle with a brutal, fanatical foe bent on our destruction. That foe controlled huge portions of Europe and denied us access to information on what was going on there. We needed that information desperately; we could not hope to win if we did not acquire intelligence on what was happening inside occupied Europe and if we did not establish contact with resistance forces there.

It was certainly possible to drop radios to people living in occupied France so they could speak to us while we sat outside the country in relative safety. This was, in fact, done on a regular basis. And it was certainly possible to pursue the acquisition of intelligence on German plans to defend France from an Allied invasion by chasing German diplomats on the cocktail circuit in neutral countries. This too was done.

It was also possible to secure intelligence through a hundred and one other methodologies, most of which were also utilized. The fact remained that, at the end of the day, if we were serious about winning the war, we needed to put people on the ground inside occupied Europe.

There was no question about what would happen to those operatives if they were caught. If they were shot promptly, they would be getting off lightly. More likely they would be beaten, tortured, cut to pieces, and tormented for weeks on end. Then they might be killed, or they might be kept alive and sent off to the death camps in Eastern Europe to die horribly a little bit at a time. No one was going to come to their rescue; no one was going to save them.

We did it anyway. We were at war, and we needed to get the job done. We did not have the luxury of limiting the level of risk or of accepting that we would not be able to find out which German divisions were in place in Normandy or what German plans were for the development of the V-2 rocket. We put our officers where they had to be under whatever cover would allow them to do their jobs. Simple. Elegant. Brutal.

In 1909 the British were faced with a crisis. The Germans had launched a huge naval building campaign. The key to British survival was the maintenance of the primacy of the British navy at sea. If this dominance was lost, and the English Channel no longer provided the protection it historically had, the future of Great Britain could be in doubt in any future military confrontation with Germany.

The British had not been particularly successful in attempts to penetrate German shipbuilding efforts. They were in the dark as to the specifications of new German warships under construction. They did not know the details of what weapons these vessels would carry.

To rectify this situation the British called on the services of Sidney Reilly, a Ukrainian-born Jew who had been in their service for a number of years and who had carried out several high-profile and very successful operations. Reilly went to work in an engineering firm in Great Britain as a welder and learned the trade. Then, disguised as a Baltic shipyard worker named Karl Hahn, Reilly traveled to Essen, Germany, and got a job at the shipyard there. Shortly thereafter he was successful in getting a job as a member of the plant's fire brigade and leveraging that access to obtain copies of the plant's schematics.[28]

Utilizing these schematics, Reilly then identified the office in the plant where the plans for the warships under construction were kept. He picked the lock to the office door, took the plans, killed a guard who surprised him in the effort, and made good his escape. After leaving the plant, Reilly went to a safe house in Dortmund, separated the plans into four pieces, and mailed each piece separately back to England. Only then did he make his own way out of Germany and back to England.[29]

Now Sidney Reilly was a lot of things, and shameless self-promoter certainly seems to have been one of them. So the reader should not draw from this example some inference that Reilly represents the very epitome of all that an intelligence officer should be. Nor should anyone walk away from an examination of this incident and miss the point that an operation that leaves a guard dead and warship plans physically missing is hardly one that we would consider to have gone as well as could be hoped. A far better op would have been one in which the plans were copied, the originals returned to their place of safekeeping, and the Germans allowed to continue busily building without any hint of the compromising of their efforts.

For our purposes the point I am attempting to make is the same as it was for the story of Virginia Hall. The British recognized that they had a pressing national security need for information on a threat. They identified what they had to do to acquire the necessary information, and they did it. It was deemed necessary to put an officer undercover inside a hostile nation and have him physically gain entry to the target shipyard. There was no other way to find out what they needed to know. Accepting that they would remain in the dark was not an option.

Let's drag the whole issue into the present day. North Korea is a hostile regime. It is, in fact, actually more aptly described as a psychotic regime, one of the most frightening and unpredictable nations on this planet. It has or is about to have nuclear weapons. What it will do with those weapons, when or how it will use them, to whom it may give them—all are largely unknown. Will a North Korean government at some point in the future threaten Japan with these weapons? Will it threaten us with them once it has developed missiles capable of reaching the United States? Will it decide in retaliation for some perceived slight by the United States to make available an atomic weapon to a terrorist organization?

I would submit that it is critical for the United States to have answers to these questions. Accepting that we do not know should not be an option. We should do whatever it takes and employ whatever methodology we need to employ to get this information. It is a simple intellectual process. Figure out what you need to know. Figure out what you need to do to get access to the information in question. Do it.

Unfortunately, as simple as that sounds, that is not, in fact, how we pursue the collection of human intelligence in today's world. In reality, we work the equation backwards. We start by accepting as a given our current organizational structure and operational approach, and then, with all of that apparently carved in stone, we try to figure out what we can and cannot acquire. Some things are just too hard. Some things are just too dangerous. We identify "intelligence gaps," meaning things we really desperately need to know but don't, and we move on.

The bulk of our intelligence officers overseas are under official cover. They wear suits, speak English, look American, and associate mostly with other diplomats and with officials of the host nation. If there is no logical reason for them to talk to someone, like, say, the leader of a local extremist group, they don't talk to him or her. If the nation to which they are posted is hostile to us, such as Venezuela, they are likely blanketed by surveillance, both technical and physical, and their movements are closely monitored.

An officer like this is not going to be able to go into Iran and gain access to a facility where a nuclear weapon is being constructed. Even more telling, he or she is not going to ever get access to anyone who works at such a facility but instead is going to sit in a friendly country outside Iran. The Iranian who is designing the bomb that will be given to Hizbullah next year, used against Tel Aviv, and start World War III is going to live in a government compound near the facility where he works. He is never going to travel outside Iran. His phones are going to be bugged and his mail read. If he is approached by someone claiming to work for American intelligence, he is probably going to think it is a test of his loyalty by his own security service and report it.

Never the twain shall meet.

We are going to recruit a guy who works in the Iranian Embassy in Country X on the other side of the world and dutifully report his opinions about what the Iranian government may or may not plan to do with nuclear weapons. We are going to report what the foreign minister of Country Y says that some Iranian official told him in a meeting last week and try to guess how reliable the info is and whether the Iranians deliberately fed it to us in the first place. We are going to combine this with blurry imagery, fragmentary SIGINT, and some informed speculation, and in the end, when the policy makers ask, we are going to show them a nice, long list of "intelligence gaps" and swear that we will do better next year.

We will not.

The problem is not sloth. There are officers all over the world pounding their heads against this problem, sweating blood and doing whatever is humanly possible. At the end of the day, though, you work with the tools you are given, and in this case and in this trade, one of those tools is your cover.

How did we get into this position? The OSS did not put all its officers under official cover worldwide and then tell them to try real hard to acquire information on Panzer divisions in France.

The Admiralty did not make Reilly a second secretary in Berlin and then ask him to see if he could penetrate a shipyard that he had no reason on earth to visit. They figured out what they needed to know, and they figured out what it was going to take to get it. They did it—they knew exactly what the risk was and what price would have to be paid, and they did it anyway.

At the end of the Second World War, we found ourselves very rapidly thrust into a worldwide confrontation with the Soviet Union. World War II was hardly ended, and the Cold War had begun. It was a massive, worldwide contest, and the CIA was a key player on our side.

We needed officers overseas: We needed them to run assets, to influence elections, to run cross-border operations. We needed lots of officers, and we needed them in place now.

Most of the places where we needed these officers were friendly to us. The West Germans were not going to spend a lot of time watching Americans. The Thais were not really going to lose a lot of sleep over what all those guys at the U.S. embassy were up to. Pretty much everything we were into was going to be compatible anyway. If we were penetrating the KGB or the local Communist Party, that was good for everybody.

So we did what seemed logical and rational. We shoveled people overseas under official cover and stuffed them all over the world. Cover was thin, but nobody cared because we figured nobody was really looking. Access was limited to the kinds of people that officially covered officers could naturally meet, but that was fine, too. We weren't looking to crawl into the guts of a terrorist group or infiltrate a drug cartel.

And for a while it all worked pretty well. The world has changed, though, and we, unfortunately, have not changed with it. If I am posted to the Middle East tomorrow, I may well go there under the same cover as an officer did thirty years ago, when the mission of the local station was to chase Russian intelligence officers. It is likely, however, that while Russians may remain targets, my primary job will be to attempt to report on what Sunni extremist groups are doing in the country where I live. How I am supposed to do that, as a white guy in a three-piece suit living in a compound surrounded by armed guards, is not necessarily clear.

Even worse, over time the institutional lash-up between the CIA and the State Department has also produced its own destructive by-product. The culture and attitudes of the department have come to permeate the CIA, to dramatically affect its mentality and limit its own tolerance for risk. Officers asked to spend a lifetime under official cover have come to live their cover all too well. The department has not become more daring, but the agency has certainly become more risk averse.

The Department of State is a critical organization. What American diplomats do worldwide on behalf of their countrymen is vastly important and, unfortunately, undervalued. In this age of preemptive action, when so many people who have never been in combat seem so eager to start wars, it would pay for us to spend considerably more time letting the diplomats try to work things out.

The job of a diplomat is to communicate and to negotiate. He must have almost infinite patience. In the face of provocation and insult, he must hold his temper; watch his words carefully; and move at a slow, deliberate pace. Caution is the rule of the day. If it takes months to decide the shape of the table at which meetings will be held or a year to finalize a list of participants at a key conference, this is to be expected. The process may be painful, but it may also save lives, avert wars, stop genocide, prevent famine.

The mind-set necessary for success as a diplomat is, however, fundamentally and dramatically different from that necessary in the world of intelligence collection. This has always been the case to some degree, but it is becoming increasingly so in today's world, where counterterrorist operations require speed and audacity. The opportunity that exists today will, if not taken, disappear tomorrow.

The OSS from the outset had confrontations with the Department of State. Many of these confrontations were resolved only as a result of the direct intervention of the president of the United States. Some of them were never resolved.

Late in the Second World War, a large number of members of the Finnish intelligence service defected from Finland and made their way to Sweden. There they provided a treasure trove of material to the local OSS station, including vast amounts of intelligence on the German military. Perhaps even more strikingly, they also offered a mountain of information on the Soviets, including several of the key Soviet codes, which the Finns had successfully broken.[30]

The OSS was elated. It was already clear that in the aftermath of the Second World War the Soviet Union would become a key adversary. Being able to read the Soviets' encrypted traffic would be a godsend. Negotiations with the Finns were begun, and an agreement was reached to acquire the codes.

At this point the Department of State entered the picture. The department was dead set against anything that had the potential to anger the Soviets, and the deal was killed. Sometime later, however, the matter resurfaced. The Finns were desperate: They were going to sell the information to someone; it was clear they would prefer to give it to the United States, but if we wouldn't take it, they would sell it elsewhere. OSS returned to the negotiating table, this time without informing the department. Donovan directed that the material be acquired immediately,[31] and it was.

Somehow the department found out about the purchase, and a protest was made directly to the president. Donovan was ordered to return the material, and incredibly, the codes were then delivered to the Soviet Embassy in Washington DC. One can only hope that before this was done, the material was copied and those copies were retained.

In late 1942 the OSS sent a two-man team high into the mountains of Tibet to make contact with the Dalai Lama. It was the height of the Second World War; the Japanese were the masters of much of Asia, and we needed all the friends we could get. The mission went extremely well. The OSS men were well received, and a basis was established for future cooperation.

The Tibetans wanted one thing, a radio transmitter. It seemed like a logical enough request. It would, among other things, allow the Tibetans to begin to push to the OSS expeditiously any and all information they might acquire about Japanese plans, intentions, and movements. Unfortunately, the Chinese became aware of the plan, and they, believing Tibet to be their sphere of influence, were not pleased.

The Department of State took the side of the Chinese and strongly opposed the provision of the transmitter. State argued that we should not provide this piece of equipment because to do so meant we would risk incurring the displeasure of the Chinese government—this at a time when large portions of China were under Japanese occupation and it was only our military and logistical support to the Chinese nationalists that was keeping them in the fight at all.[32]

Fortunately, in this case the OSS prevailed. The transmitter was sent and arrived in Tibet in late 1943. The foundation of future American intelligence cooperation with the Tibetans had been laid.

When approached to provide cover for an OSS station in Istanbul during the Second World War, the State Department was initially highly resistant, arguing that "the discovery by the Turkish government that the Foreign Service was being used as a shield for undercover intelligence work could not but have the most unfortunate results".[33] Moreover, the department argued that the OSS presence was unnecessary and that State officers could acquire all necessary information. Ultimately, the department relented and allowed the establishment of a station, but it still refused to provide cover for individual officers. OSS personnel had to utilize the cover of a host of other wartime agencies to facilitate their operations.

The mind-set of the department has not changed over time. Just as during the war State was fixated on the risk of angering our allies the Soviets and the Chinese, it remains today opposed across the board to any action that might displease other nations with whom we have friendly dealings. Given the nature of the political situation in the Middle East, where even our key "allies" in the war on terror are attempting to avoid coming down too firmly in opposition to Sunni extremism, this effectively places State in the role of opposing any strong, decisive action by intelligence organizations against terrorist cells in the region.

Several years ago I was serving as the chief of station in a Middle Eastern country. There was a sizable American presence in country, and there was also a growing number of Sunni extremists and a steady drumbeat of threat reporting about plans for attacks on U.S. targets in country. Terrorist attacks occurred with frequency in neighboring nations, and the possibility of a catastrophic attack on Americans in the nation where I was assigned was a very real possibility.

At one point we acquired a series of very concrete reports showing that we were in the run-up to a specific attack. Material had been procured by key extremists; targets had been chosen. It might be days or it might be weeks, but an attack was coming. The details we had in our possession suggested that casualties might be massive.

Throughout this time frame, as required, I kept the ambassador informed of all reporting. I also kept him informed of the status of our planning for operations to disrupt these attacks. The ambassador was the chief of mission. No action could or would be taken to prevent the attacks without his approval.

At the conclusion of one such meeting with the ambassador, after I had outlined one possible course of action that would result in the detention and imprisonment of the individual directing the attack planning, the ambassador looked at me and advised that he was opposed to any such action and that he would always be opposed to any such action. Just to make sure I fully understood the strength of his opposition, he then went on to say that before he would ever agree to support the type of operation I had described, he would allow the attack to take place. He stated that he would accept the loss of American lives before he would knowingly invite the kind of political fallout in our relations with the host country that the contemplated preemptive operation would entail.

I was, to say the least, flabbergasted. I was not necessarily wedded to the idea of undertaking the operation I had described. I certainly had no illusions about its ease of execution. Nor did I disagree with the ambassador regarding the potential political fallout. I could not help but wonder, however, if the ambassador's willingness to knowingly allow Americans to die would still hold if it were members of his own family who would be the targets.

This ambassador was a good man. He was a dedicated public servant who had spent the better part of his life deployed to unpleasant locales doing his best to serve the interests of his nation. He believed with all his heart that he was doing what was in the best interest of the United States of America. Somehow, that all led him to the point where he was willing to argue against taking immediate, decisive action and for allowing a terrorist plot to proceed and Americans to die.

All embassies abroad run in roughly the same fashion, based on the country-team concept. The ambassador is the chief of mission—he runs the show. The country team, which comprises the heads of all the agencies represented in country, works for him. This includes the chief of station. While the ambassador does not necessarily delve into the details of all operations in country, he makes the call on anything of real significance. No action against a terrorist cell, for example, is going to happen without the ambassador's approval. Even if the COS is the most aggressive, forward-leaning officer in the DO, his ability to act is going to be dependent in large measure on the amount of risk the ambassador is willing to accept.

Most ambassadors are, not surprisingly, less than enthused about the possibility of having the work of the department derailed by an agency op that goes bad. The ambassador is not really charged with ensuring that the CIA succeeds in disrupting terrorist operations or penetrates drug cartels. The ambassador is answerable to the department for things like the success of ongoing free-trade negotiations. The last thing on earth the ambassador wants is a monkey wrench thrown into the works by some wild-eyed CIA officer hell-bent on taking down Sunni extremists.

The really disastrous impact on the CIA is, however, what this relationship with State does to the culture of the agency itself. It is not simply that the department stymies the CIA in its efforts to pursue targets. Much more serious is the fact that over time this relationship results in the CIA itself becoming more and more attuned to the department's way of thinking. The CIA begins to engage in self-censorship. Ideas and proposals never make it to the ambassador because they are killed internally before they ever get to that stage.

A CIA station in country is essentially completely dependent on the goodwill of the ambassador for its continued existence. The number-one priority of any COS is to maintain a good relationship with his ambassador. A good working relationship is golden; a negative one may be the kiss of death.

Ambassadors who are not pleased with the performance of the COS are not generally shy about complaining to Washington. Such complaints, once relayed from Main State, the State Department headquarters in DC to CIA headquarters, are taken very seriously. The CIA has no choice but to respond immediately to any indication that a COS is not towing the line. Even a hint of displeasure from the ambassador is enough to result in an immediate message from a division chief to the COS telling him to fix the problem and put things back on track. In only the rarest and most egregious of circumstances will headquarters be willing to buck the department and support action in opposition to the desires of the ambassador in country.

The guidance to a COS is clear: Do not rock the boat. Do not make waves. Keep on the good side of the ambassador. Make him happy.

The lash-up with State impacts directly on individual CIA officers as well. If you spend your life overseas living and working under official cover, that existence begins to color your perceptions. The norms and expectations of other American officials abroad begin to become your norms. You accept constraints on your behavior and your psychology. You no longer think in wide-open terms of how best to accomplish the mission; instead you begin your analysis of any problem by framing the issue in terms of what is acceptable within this broader official culture.

Perhaps even more disastrously, however, the workforce of the DO as a whole has come to expect that a career in the CIA means living under official cover and following a trajectory similar to that of other non-CIA American officials abroad. There is no law that says that CIA officers should only be subject to the same level of risk as their State colleagues. There is no real driving necessity that espionage should only be practiced by individuals living abroad under official cover, accompanied by their dependents and rotating roughly every two to three years from one city to another. We have, however, made that the norm, and after many decades of doing so, we have created an entire organization staffed by persons who joined the service and remained in its employ with the expectation that this norm would be unchanged.

We began this chapter by talking about the mind-set employed by the original OSS. As noted, that mind-set might in many ways be characterized as being very straightforward, even simple. Identify what you need to do to acquire the information critical to national security, and do it. Simple.

Simple does not mean easy. Simple does not mean painless. When you send an officer into occupied France disguised as a peasant woman, you know that there is a very real chance she will not come back. You understand that she may die and that this death may be horrible. At the very least, you know that the officer will spend long months separated from family and friends, living by her wits and unable, ever, to fully relax or reveal herself.

These kinds of risks have existed from the beginning of time. Espionage has always been a dangerous game. It is not clean. It is not antiseptic. Like combat, espionage inevitably involves casualties. You can't change this, any more than you can expect to go to war and not suffer losses.

We have largely lost this understanding, and we have ceased to function based on what is required to get the job done. We have simply decided that we will not subject ourselves to the level of risk required to accomplish many of the missions before us.

In the 1990s I arrived at a station in Asia to begin an assignment. I was primarily focused on the pursuit of terrorist targets and on chasing Iranians and Iraqis. This meant a significant level of risk, and one of the first things I did was inquire of the COS as to his policy on firearms and managing high-risk meetings.

The COS responded by saying that there were no firearms in station. He noted that his first official act as COS, after arrival in country, had been to have all firearms crated up and sent home. His opinion was very straightforward: If we identified an operation that could not be conducted safely without the use of firearms, we should not conduct the operation. There were as far as he was concerned no circumstances under which it was worth the risk to place one of our officers in physical jeopardy.

Let me be clear: I am in no particular hurry to get shot. I have spent large chunks of my life evading efforts to kill me. I am very happy to have done so successfully up to this point. Bleeding out on a filthy sidewalk in a third-world country surrounded by flies and refuse does not strike me as either dramatic or memorable. Nor am I advocating that intelligence operations ought to turn into the kind of "shoot 'em up" cartoon images so common in Hollywood productions. An intelligence officer's job is to get the information he was sent for, ideally without being detected, and get home. If you are in a gunfight, you've probably failed in your mission.

That said, I remember vividly the thoughts I had when the COS in the story above explained his philosophy to me. I wondered by what authority we had decided to arbitrarily limit the level of risk we would accept. I wondered who exactly was going to do the really risky operations if it was not the CIA. I wondered why it was okay to allow terrorist organizations to continue to operate and innocent civilians to die but not okay to expect a trained intelligence officer to put his hide on the line every now and then.

What I am suggesting here is that we have crossed a critical psychological divide. We began with an organization, the OSS, composed of individuals who understood and accepted as a basic element of their employment that they were expected to put their lives on the line. We have ended up with an organization in which significant numbers of individuals believe that they are entitled to put in their twenty years moving from one large city to another, subject to no risk other than the chance of being declared persona non grata and asked to return to CONUS a few months early. Arguably, in some cases, these individuals are no longer pretending to be something other than intelligence officers—they *are* something else.

There are, of course, officers who are not under official cover. There is also, as has been reported widely in the press, a move to significantly increase the numbers of such officers. Much of what needs to be discussed on this topic is not appropriate for an unclassified medium such as this, but I think a number of the key issues concerning nonofficially covered officers (NOCs) are the same as those identified above.

NOCs are probably the key to the future of the CIA. The effective, widespread use of such officers would really represent a return to the roots of espionage and its traditional method of practice. Reilly would certainly be characterized as an NOC. Most of the OSS officers who operated on a long-term basis inside occupied Europe were also NOCs.

If the CIA is going to move in this direction, though, it needs to address two key factors. First, NOCs cannot simply be an adjunct to officially covered operations. If the bulk of officers remain "inside" and NOC operations are merely a sideshow, then nothing has fundamentally changed. In other words the challenge here is not just to layer NOC operations on top of an existing, outdated edifice. The challenge is to morph the organization into something fundamentally different from the ground up.

We need an organization in which officers exist abroad under whatever cover facilitates the mission. Period. The entire concept of an organization in which the norm is for officers to exist under official cover and to live a lifestyle through their whole careers needs to be abandoned. What we need in its place is an entity that places its officers abroad in whatever status they need to allow them access to the targets against which they must operate.

Second, and in line with the point made above, the basic approach to the conduct of CIA operations has to change. If I take an officially covered officer out of country and replace him with an officer living out in town under commercial cover, this is a good start. However, if I am still constrained in the use of this new officer by the same risk-averse mind-set, I probably have not gained very much.

Consider the question of penetration of terrorist organizations. An officially covered officer in a city in an Arab nation may, in fact, have great difficulty in getting access to targets of interest with information on terrorist activities. An officer under nonofficial cover as a local businessman may much more readily make contact with the kinds of individuals we need to recruit.

To fully exploit the access afforded by nonofficial cover, however, we are going to have to accept a much higher level of risk. Our ethnic Arab officer under nonofficial cover may meet targets of interest at mosque. He may be approached to help with extremist activities, provide financial support, move material and equipment, or any of a number of other things. In the process, however, he is going to be terribly exposed. If his loyalties are suspect, if he slips up, if information leaks, he is dead. There will be no diplomatic protest. He will not be given forty-eight hours to pack his household effects. His comms will go dead. He will miss his scheduled contact with his inside officer. We will find his body by the road outside town, or we will receive the video of his beheading in the mail.

We have walked this path before. The OSS was created to fight a dirty shadow war against a terrible enemy bent on our destruction. Certainly, the brutality of the Nazi regime, which engineered the systematic elimination of entire peoples, exceeded that of even our current adversaries. But we won the war against Hitler, and we can win this one. We can't do that, though, by clinging to the outdated, calcified structure created to fight the Cold War. The rules have changed, and the gloves are off. We need to return to our roots and follow suit.

CHAPTER FOUR

Define Elite

SHORTLY AFTER I JOINED THE CIA, I WAS SENT TO AN AGENCY training facility to undergo a number of weeks of paramilitary training. During this time I was instructed in the use of firearms, high-speed driving, methodologies for evading ambush, land navigation, and a host of other disciplines. In general, it was not only excellent training but a lot of fun, sort of like all the best parts of being in the military without the usual Mickey Mouse bullshit that often went with being in uniform.

As part of our training, we got up every morning, fell into formation, and did physical training. We did push-ups, pull-ups, sit-ups, and so on and then went for a run of several miles in formation before showering and heading to chow. Again, for anyone who had been in the military, which was a significant portion of my class, this was all old hat.

I discovered after training began that this paramilitary training, once the exclusive preserve of operational personnel, had now been opened up to officers from across the agency. This was part of a move underway at the time to break down barriers and build a more "inclusive" organization. Although I didn't realize it at the time, for most of the people in the DO, it was the latest move in an ongoing war against the Clandestine Service.

My class had a number of ops officers in it. It also had communicators, logistics officers, open-source specialists, and administrative personnel. While quite a few of the ops officers were prior service, many of these other individuals were not. They arrived at the training facility without any experience in such an environment, and many of them were hopelessly out of shape as well.

During our very first run in formation, the guy next to me in ranks, a communicator and computer expert, fell out after only a few hundred meters and started walking. I dropped out of formation, ran back to him, and made him start running again. Then I stayed with him, following the formation and encouraging him to keep going. A buddy of mine who was calling cadence repeatedly ran the entire formation in a loop and swung it back around to pick up the straggling communicator. Many of the men and women in ranks yelled encouragement. The communicator was hurting; he was in terrible shape.

But he didn't quit. He sucked it up and kept moving.

We repeated that same performance almost every morning for a couple of weeks. The communicator kept at it. He was making progress; he was getting better. It wasn't pretty, and he wasn't going to set land-speed records anytime soon, but before long he was going to be able to keep up with the formation.

Then something happened. The communicator noticed that there was another individual in the platoon who also dropped out of formation every day—only this individual did not try to keep up. He just stopped running and walked the rest of the way through physical training. He made no effort to improve his performance, and most telling of all, nothing happened.

The instructors whom we had for paramilitary training were for the most part former military special operations folks of some ilk: Seals, Green Berets, Force Recon, and the like. They were world class. But they made no effort of any kind to push the individual who dropped out and walked every morning. They took no action against this individual and in essence just acted like they couldn't see what was going on.

At some point in this exercise, I pulled one of the instructors aside and asked him what was going on. What was the point of doing PT if no standards were going to be enforced? Didn't everyone have to take and pass some sort of physical fitness test of some kind? How were we supposed to keep people like the communicator, who were trying hard to improve themselves, motivated if they saw that there was no consequence to simply stacking arms?

The instructor I was talking to was a former Army Ranger and a Vietnam combat vet. He didn't really need me to tell him things were screwed up. That said, he took the time to explain to me what was going on. He noted that there was a strong sentiment within many portions of the agency that the DO was too elitist and too insular. The move was afoot to change this, to break down barriers, to let everyone who wanted it to have a shot at getting involved operationally. He noted that when many of the non-DO components in the CIA had been told to select individuals to go to paramilitary training, they had expressed concern that physical fitness testing and standards might disadvantage their folks. Accordingly, while testing would still be done, and individuals would still be "encouraged" to engage in PT, failure to pass a PT test would no longer mean you did not pass the course.

In short, the training had been neutered. You could sweat blood or you could stroll through the tough parts. In the end everybody would be treated the same, and we would all feel better about the new, kinder, gentler CIA.

Shortly thereafter, the communicator began to backslide. He quit trying. Eventually, I gave up even trying to encourage him to keep up. He may have been in marginally better shape at the end of the class than he was at the beginning but only marginally. He had learned the most important lesson: There were no standards.

This is how they did it when the OSS was formed: Personnel who were brought into the OSS were brought to Washington DC and processed administratively for a few days. Paperwork was taken care of; other basic bureaucratic necessities were satisfied. Then everybody was thrown into a truck or a jeep and taken to the first of what would probably be several training camps.[34]

At this camp, which was located on the grounds of what had been the Congressional Country Club, OSS personnel were housed in tents and Quonset huts. Intensive evaluation and screening of individuals was conducted while training on a host of subjects took place. Physical training began early and often continued late. Trainees ran; they negotiated obstacle courses; they climbed ropes; they did long, difficult compass courses in daylight and at night.

Personnel at the camp also trained in the use of a wide variety of weapons. They practiced ambushes. They learned the art of infiltration.

Then they moved on to the next camp. Things got tougher. Intensive training in hand-to-hand combat was conducted. Field exercises continued. Tradecraft instruction was added to the mix. They worked with explosives and were taught communication skills. Training days started early and ended late. Individuals who couldn't hack it were sent home.[35]

The exact sequence and content of training varied slightly over time. Some individuals, depending on their assignment, received more or less of some particular skill. The OSS was an organization being started from scratch in the middle of a war. As lessons were learned, training was modified. Sometimes, when operational requirements dictated, training was truncated. Max Corvo never finished his; he was pulled out early and put to work recruiting personnel for work in Italy.[36] Consistently, however, the training was demanding and tough, and while the OSS tended to have a loose definition of "discipline," there was a serious, no-nonsense approach to the work being done. Everyone understood that this was for real. The skills being learned were going to be put to use very soon.

At the conclusion of training, most personnel were put through a practical exercise. This was usually conducted outside a training facility and required trainees to acquire actual intelligence on targets of potential significance to the war effort, such as steel plants, automobile factories, and the like. The goal was to force the personnel to demonstrate a basic mastery of the skills they had been taught.

One OSS officer named Erasmus Kloman was assigned, along with three partners, to penetrate the steel plants in Pittsburgh. Their three-part mission was to penetrate one or more plants, to observe and report on activities there, and to plan a sabotage attack.[37] Kloman's specific target was the McKeesport plant of the National Pipe and Tube Company in Elwood City, northwest of Pittsburgh.

Kloman, operating under an assumed name, rented a room in Elwood City and then went to the employment officer for the plant, assuming that in wartime he would have no difficulty in being hired. To his surprise he found that the plant was adhering to procedure and would require him to submit to a full security background check before he could be considered for employment. His plan had crashed and burned, and he was back to square one. An added pressure was that the other members of his team were doing well and moving ahead with collection of information on their targets.

Desperate to succeed, Kloman cased the perimeter of the McKeesport plant and succeeded in identifying a gap in the chain-link fence. On the last night of his "mission," he entered the plant, located management offices in a secure area, and made off with a sizeable number of sensitive documents and plant plans. Examination in Washington later showed that these documents could have been of significant use to the enemy. National Pipe and Tube was instructed to beef up security, and Kloman became somewhat of a celebrity within OSS. [38]

There is nothing magic about the exact methodology used by the OSS in training its personnel. Looking back on it now, decades later, one can see that initially significant portions of it were thrown together rather haphazardly. As noted earlier, the OSS was blazing a new trail. No one knew exactly how to put together a program to train members of a clandestine human intelligence-collection organization—the United States had never constructed such a thing before. With time, though, there was refinement: Some elements of the training were scrapped, and some were strengthened.

It should also be said that if we were to design such a training program now, from the ground up, it is likely that we would put emphasis on a different mix of skills from those the OSS did. For example, it may not be quite so important for intelligence officers today to know as much about derailing locomotives as did the OSS. It may be much more important for them to have a strong grounding in the science of chemical, biological, radiological, and nuclear weapons.

The most important thing about the OSS training program for the purposes of our discussion, though, is what it did to forge the individuals who went through it into a team. Some of the people who came through the program, particularly those who went on to form Jedburgh teams, which jumped into France after D-Day, or those who were members of operational groups directing guerrilla groups deep in enemy territory, were legitimately world class in their command of military and paramilitary skills. Others, such as Kloman, received a thorough grounding but probably didn't surpass the average infantry officer in their levels of military knowledge.

All the trainees, however, had proved something to themselves and to each other. They entered as individuals, but they left as members of an elite organization. They had confidence in themselves, and they had confidence in each other. They were welded together as a team, with a common understanding of what was expected of them and what tests they had passed to gain entrance to the OSS. Wherever they went, whatever they were called upon to do, they knew they could depend on each other.

Once operational personnel have completed paramilitary training in today's CIA, they go on to be trained at length in tradecraft and operational procedures. This course, which is of some significant duration, is effective and thorough. It is, however, a trade school. It teaches students basic skills as individuals. It does not include any physical component, and it is not designed to build unit cohesion or esprit de corps. It is a long, hard slog, but each student goes through it as an individual, and frankly, anyone who is willing to put in the time and effort to learn the skills is going to come out the other end certified for operational work.

Anyone who has gone through a rigorous military training course of any kind will understand precisely what has been lost from our training of operational personnel. If you go to Ranger School and sweat blood for weeks on end, all you live for is the end of training. When the end comes, though, and you pin on the Ranger tab, you know that you have accomplished something. You know you have proved something to yourself and to others. You also know, when you work with fellow Rangers, that they have had to get over the same bar and that you can count on them to perform at a very high level under extreme circumstances.

I went through agency paramilitary training. With me in that training were former Army Rangers, Marine officers, and at least one former foreign military officer. These individuals were superb and capable of going anywhere and operating under virtually any conditions. I also went through training with individuals who could not successfully negotiate an obstacle course, never finished a run, and got lost on every orienteering course. We did not leave as a team with a common understanding of our capabilities. We left as individuals, each man or woman carrying a mental short list of those officers he or she would work with and those to avoid like the plague.

What has happened to the training of operational personnel is, unfortunately, only one piece of what I described earlier as a war on the Clandestine Service. There have been a number of other, even more damaging steps taken that, collectively, have brought us to the current state of crisis in our human collection capability.

In the early 1990s the Clinton Administration effectively decided to declare the world safe for democracy. The Cold War was over, and terrorism was not judged to be a significant threat. The CIA's budget was slashed, and recruitment plummeted. There is no way to discuss this topic in the detail it deserves in an unclassified setting, but let it suffice to say for our purposes here that we came perilously close at points prior to the attacks on 11 September 2001 to shutting down the pipeline of new hires—the lifeblood of any organization—into the Clandestine Service. Training classes were conducted less frequently than ever before, and they were reduced to a fraction of their former size.

The world, of course, did not really become a less dangerous place just because Bill Clinton decided to say it had. The threats continued to multiply, and CIA stations continued to be required to report on these threats. Sometimes, because hiring of ops officers had been so dramatically reduced, stations just went without officers and worked shorthanded. Increasingly, though, in order to fill slots and keep moving, the Directorate of Operations began to draw on personnel from other parts of the organization. Individuals with no ops training were crossed over into the Clandestine Service and put into ops slots. It was a desperate measure, but these were desperate times.

The bulk of these individuals were good, hardworking, patriotic Americans. They wanted to serve their country and to do something of value; their motives can only be applauded. This does not change the fact, though, that they were for the most part untrained and were individuals who had originally been recruited to do very different jobs from those they were now called upon to do. Not everyone can be an effective CIA ops officer any more than everyone can be a successful trial lawyer or a physician. It takes a special set of skills, and designating someone to serve in an operational slot does not automatically confer these abilities upon that person.

The appointment of John Deutsch as director of the CIA and his designation of Nora Slotkin as the executive director took this trend to a new low point. Both Deutsch and Slotkin made it crystal clear that they found the performance of the DO to be severely lacking and that they considered its insular, elitist culture to be a major part of the reason. Ms. Slotkin, in particular, went out of her way to be combative in this approach, dismissing and disciplining significant numbers of officers for perceived failures and repeatedly signaling her displeasure with the culture of the DO. During this time frame the agency even began to send out as chiefs of station nonoperational personnel, appointing, for example, Directorate of Intelligence (DI) analysts to be COSs abroad.

Maybe the significance, both real and symbolic, of this move is not immediately clear to people not steeped in the culture of the DO. To put it in context, it would be tantamount to naming an officer from, say, the Army Transportation Corps as the commanding general of an infantry division. I don't mean that comparison as a slap at DI analysts, who are crucial members of the CIA structure. I mean it as a reflection of the fact that an analyst, no matter how bright and capable, does not begin to have the background and experience to run a station.

The COS has, as alluded to earlier, a host of jobs he has to perform. His single most critical function, however, is to ensure that intelligence operations in his country are conducted securely and safely. He has to be the ultimate judge of what is and is not done and how all operations are conducted. A mistake may mean a diplomatic incident. It may mean a political crisis. Or it may mean that people die.

As I have said, the COS does not have to be the best ops officer in his station. He does, however, have to be competent, and he does have to have significant operational experience. Just as the commanding general of an infantry division has to have a thorough grounding in infantry tactics, the COS has to know how to run an op. He has to have handled assets. He has to have made difficult recruitments. He has to have the sixth sense that goes with being a solid, experienced ops officer.

A COS who does not possess this level of experience is incapable of doing his job. He is a general who's never been in combat, a ship captain who has never been to sea. No matter how bright and how well intentioned, he is crippled and reduced to relying upon others to tell him what to do.

This is not rocket science; this is baseline common sense. The fact that it was not recognized is shocking and indicative of how completely out of touch with the realities of operational work agency management had become in this time frame.

The broader message that these appointments were intended to convey was not lost on the workforce. As senior operational assignments were handed out to nonoperational personnel and the ranks of the DO filled with former logistics officers and ex-secretaries, everyone understood what was being said: There is nothing special about the DO. Anyone can do this job. Elitism is the problem.

I don't know Ms. Slotkin. I will give her the benefit of the doubt and assume that when she took the actions she did she had the best interests of the country at heart. I suspect she looked at a DO that was not getting the job done against hard targets; found it, in her view, obstructionist; and decided the answer was to break it down. In doing so, however, in my opinion, she took precisely the wrong direction and only succeeded in making an already bad situation worse.

If we turned around tomorrow and found that the United States Marine Corps could no longer do its job effectively, we would investigate the reasons, and we would take corrective action. Likely we would find that such corrective action meant a renewed focus on standards, on discipline, and on performance. I submit that such corrective action would be highly unlikely to involve bringing in officers from the Coast Guard to take charge of Marine infantry battalions. No matter how capable such officers might be, they would have no idea how to operate in their new positions. The mere fact of their appointment would have its own destructive impact as well. A corps grounded in an understanding of its own elite status would hear loud and clear that it was no longer considered to be anything special.

Unfortunately, as destructive as all the moves outlined above were, they were not the end of developments that undermined the DO.

The cost of living in Washington DC has been rising exponentially for years. All government agencies trying to retain personnel have felt the pressure from this. It is not too much to say that at times the CIA has literally not been able to pay enough to enable qualified junior officers to remain on the payroll. Upon his return to CONUS from an overseas posting, possibly the single best DI analyst and targeteer I know was forced to send his wife and children to live with relatives in another state while he served a headquarters posting. He could not afford to support them in the DC Metro area.

CIA personnel are paid on the General Schedule (GS) scale; they receive no special pay. If you are a GS-12 in the CIA, you make exactly what a GS-12 in the Department of Agriculture makes. It is not a lot, and it is probably not nearly enough to support a family comfortably in DC. Consequently, if you want to retain people in the service, the pressure is intense to promote them as fast as you can in order to get them more money.

Post-9/11, this already intense pressure became even worse. We went into the "war on terror" shorthanded and behind the curve. We could not possibly afford to lose more people at the same time that we were expanding operations, standing up new stations and bases, and taking on new missions. Somebody had to run these new operations, and in many cases there was no one to do that other than new hires or people who had been brought into the DO from other directorates. We promoted them as fast as we could.

The result was not hard to predict. It was now possible to have a Chief of Station in a critical area who had been on board only a few years. He might be a very capable man, but the fact remained that he was still at the stage in his career where he should have been learning at the feet of a much more seasoned officer. The officer running a branch in station might very well be a former polygrapher who had converted to the DO and been promoted rapidly to fill a void. He would likely be a good, hardworking, well-intentioned individual who had never met an asset, never made a recruitment, and never written an intelligence report. His desire to serve his country notwithstanding, he would be highly unlikely to have any idea how to penetrate al-Qaeda operations or what guidance to give a first-tour officer on how to handle a difficult recruitment.

Back at headquarters all these factors were combined with yet another dynamic, the creation of a class of "ops officers" who had never been overseas and never intended to serve down range. Regardless of that, these individuals were pushed upward into ever-more-significant and more-powerful positions, from which they were charged with the direction and orchestration of operations worldwide. The gulf between the field and headquarters, which always exists in any organization of any size, became a chasm.

As the agency expanded post-9/11, its culture was no longer anything close to that of the OSS. Where once there had been a common understanding of expectations and a willingness to follow orders and undertake any assignment, there was now a much softer, less disciplined structure. Within the organization, to be sure, there remained highly capable officers who believed it was their duty to serve where and when they were needed. There were also large numbers of individuals who had never been trained as ops officers but were now serving in ops slots and who had joined the organization with very different expectations of what they would be expected to do. While some individuals remained willing to jump on an aircraft at a moment's notice and deploy as needed, many others viewed the agency simply as just another federal job.

One individual who I think embodies what I am trying to convey is a finance officer with whom I served in the late 1990s.

He arrived in station about a year into my tour and from the outset made clear that he did not believe that he was part of the operational mission of the office. He stated repeatedly that he worked from nine to five, and that was it. If we did not get to him between these hours, we were out of luck.

One day in station we were hit with a short-fuse requirement. It was late in the day, and it was clear we were going to need to dispense funds that evening. While we were still trying to sort out exactly how much we would need, I called in the finance officer. It was shortly before five, and I gave him a heads-up that he was going to need to stick around and be prepared to work late.

The finance officer refused. He told me he was going home at five; if we got to him before then, he would help. If not, we were out of luck.

I lost it. I told him that he would stay as long as he needed to stay. I told him we had a job to do, that he was part of a team, and that when he came to station he accepted the necessity to do whatever it took to get the job done. Serving down range as an ops officer was never really a job to me. It was a calling, as it always has been to those who really believe in the mission. The brazenness with which an officer could simply dismiss any interest in mission accomplishment infuriated me.

The finance officer did not back down. He responded that he had not joined to be involved in ops. He said he understood that I was required to work long hours but noted that, in his opinion, he had not joined to work nights or weekends. He then left my office and went to talk to the COS, with whom he lodged a complaint because I had raised my voice and been "mean" to him.

This individual was not disciplined, and he was not dismissed. I saw him at headquarters the day before I retired. He now runs a large finance section and oversees support to several field stations. I assume he continues to treat his service in the CIA as simply another nine to five job, one that requires little if any sacrifice. In all likelihood he could just as well serve in any of a hundred other federal agencies without feeling any real difference.

This officer, unfortunately, is not an exception. He is simply a good example of what has become all too commonplace. Once upon a time those who ran operations in the CIA treated that profession almost as one might treat membership in a priesthood or some other order. It was not a job. It was your life. It was all consuming, and the only measure of how much to give was how much it took to get the job done. That world has ceased to exist.

In the current climate it has become largely completely voluntary for officers to agree to serve down range in the war zones and crisis zones of the world. Many, probably the vast majority, do and volunteer particularly to go to war zones and denied areas where the operational challenges are huge. Unfortunately, many others decide that serving overseas is not for them and elect to work in "operational" positions at headquarters as a career. The rush to push everyone upward in rank as fast as possible carries them along, too. It is now not only possible to have a very green officer serving in the field as a COS; it is possible to have an extremely inexperienced officer—and potentially one never trained as an ops officer—serving as the head of a large, important headquarters group overseeing ops in a number of different countries.

Add to this the impact of the ongoing exodus of experienced operations officers from the DO, many of them generally fed up with the disintegration of the organization, and you have a true crisis. It is not simply that junior personnel, some with no training, most with little or no experience, are being pushed upward at a ferocious pace, it is that there is no one left at any level to guide them or give them advice. The number of senior intelligence service officers in the organization is capped at a relatively low level; below that, with few exceptions, every GS-15 officer who hits retirement age is walking out the door. There is no institutional memory, no tribal lore.

I retired at the end of May 2008. Shortly after my retirement I was asked to consider taking a position inside the CIA as a senior ops advisor for a large headquarters operational component. Although I really had already begun to focus on moving in another direction professionally, I went to headquarters to meet with the individuals running the program in question and to get some additional information.

What they described to me was an initiative in which they were actively searching for retired senior ops officers and placing them into each major operational command at the front-office level. The entire purpose of this endeavor was to bring in individuals with seasoning and experience to provide counsel and guidance to the increasingly junior and inexperienced staff officers serving in headquarters management positions. In other words, to compensate for the fact that they no longer had people on staff who knew what they were doing, they were creating a group of "advisors" who would attempt to provide on-the-job training and counsel.

It was, as headquarters initiatives go, a worthy endeavor. I ultimately declined the offer for personal reasons, but I have to admit I felt a little guilty about doing so. I was at the same time, however, stunned. I spent a lot of years in the agency, and as this manuscript makes clear, I have seen a lot of bad things happen. Still, I really found it very hard to fathom how an organization could continue to push experienced ops officers out the door and promote folks with no qualifications to senior positions and then think that it could fix the resulting disaster by hiring a handful of contractors and telling them to teach "the kids" what they need to know. It struck me as the functional equivalent of putting a Band-Aid on a sucking chest wound.

This overall decline in standards for operational personnel has extended to language capability as well. This has been, of course, a weakness within the CIA for many years, but recent trends have exaggerated the problem and turned what was previously a bad situation into a true crisis. My last PCS posting abroad prior to retirement was as COS in a Middle Eastern nation. During the bulk of my time there, while we were engaged heavily against terrorist and extremist targets, I did not have a single qualified Arabic linguist in my entire shop.

The OSS dealt with the issue of language ability and area knowledge in a very straightforward fashion. It went out and recruited native speakers. If you look at the names of the individuals in the stories in this book, you will see graphic evidence of that. The men on the ground in Greece were mostly Greek-American. The teams operating deep inside Yugoslavia were often composed of Serbs or Croats. When the OSS could not find native speakers, it chose to recruit largely individuals like Virginia Hall who had lived and worked abroad for large portions of their adult lives and could readily blend into the local citizenry.

In the early years of the CIA, there began to be a move away from this tendency, due largely to CI concerns. Donovan had often been criticized for a lack of rigor in this regard and was accused of allowing Communists to join OSS. As the Cold War ensued, there was a strong focus on preventing this kind of penetration.

The CIA, however, in these early years often compensated for this fact by allowing individuals to spend long periods of time posted to individual nations and rotating them inside fairly small geographic regions. I served early on in my career with an officer who had spent more than ten consecutive years on the ground in the same European nation. Language was considered important, and many officers in the early years were gifted linguists.

As the years passed, however, and the organization began to stagnate and calcify, language became more and more of an afterthought. Officers were still sent to language school and formally expected to demonstrate some level of proficiency. In practice, however, there was no real penalty for failing to test out at a satisfactory level. In any event, those officers who did "pass" the tests at the end of training were then sent to postings under official cover, where they rarely used their language skills for more than routine tasks. The CIA became an organization composed of marginal linguists with limited or no capability to interact at any real level of sophistication with the bulk of the non-English-speaking population in any particular country.

Early on in my career, I was assigned to a European nation and put to work against the terrorist target. My immediate superior was an officer with several tours who had just completed a full year of training in the language of the nation in question. Shortly after his arrival in country, he and I and some other ops officers went out after work to a local restaurant for dinner.

My new boss, I guess in order to demonstrate that he was in charge, took the lead in ordering for the entire group. He could not do it.

After a full year of intensive language training at huge expense to the taxpayers, he was incapable of ordering a simple meal and a few beers. He fumbled around, and the waiter made clear his complete lack of comprehension. After several painful minutes, I jumped in and explained what we wanted. I did not consider myself a brilliant linguist, but realistically a few weeks of listening to language tapes at home should have been enough to bring most people to a level where they could have handled the conversation in question.

My boss clearly had absorbed virtually nothing from his many months of instruction. It didn't matter; he was sent out to his next assignment anyway.

On this occasion lack of language ability was embarrassing and inconvenient. In many other instances, it is much more than that. About midway through my career, I was working at a post in the Middle East where we were heavily engaged against our target. One of the sources we ran was a military officer who was reported to have direct access to surface-to-surface missile units. He had managed to slip away from his post few times a year to meet with us and be debriefed. The intelligence he provided was of critical importance, and to ensure we got it right, we brought in an officer with Arabic language proficiency to meet with this source whenever he could make it out of country.

On one occasion about halfway through my tour in this Middle Eastern country, we were alerted that the source would be coming out, requested the Arabic-speaking officer TDY to our location and were informed that due to personal family issues he was unable to travel. We were on our own. I was handed the case and told to come up with a solution.

With a great deal of effort, I located a native Arabic speaker in a neighboring station who was available to TDY to our station to assist. This individual was not an ops officer; he was at the neighboring location working as a translator and reviewing Arabic-language documents. I believed, however, that with his Arabic and my ops experience we could work together as a team and handle the meeting with the source.

Fortunately, this arrangement worked. The translator listened carefully to my guidance and made sure the source understood that I was in charge. As a team we pulled off the meeting successfully. In the process, however, we also determined that we did not have a case.

Huge portions of the reporting from this source were wrong, starting with the asset's name. He did not have any intelligence on surface-to-surface missiles, nor did he have any access to that target. His information concerned surface-to-air missiles, something entirely different, and that intelligence was acquired indirectly through subsources of dubious reliability. Maybe most importantly, our asset was no longer on active duty, having retired a number of years earlier.

Our "Arabic speaking" case officer, who had been handling the case for a long period of time, had gotten almost nothing right. It was clear that his language ability, billed as near native, was marginal at best and that he had nothing near the level of fluency necessary to handle an asset in his native language. The entire case was a debacle, and I said so loudly and clearly in my reporting.

This already bad situation in regard to language capability has been exaggerated and aggravated by every development in the last few years. Not only do we still have fully certified ops officers serving in operational posts who have no significant language ability, but we have former logs officers, polygraphers, analysts, and secretaries who have moved into operational posts without language training of any kind. Most of these individuals in point of fact have no demonstrated aptitude for learning foreign languages. Even if we were to undertake some massive effort to educate them, it is unlikely that most of them would be able to acquire any significant level of proficiency in any event.

The days when we required our officers to acquire significant regional expertise and to perfect the language skills they may have developed have also come and gone. Officers rotate among assignments rapidly. They punch tickets and then hurry home to stand near the flagpole and get promoted. Many of them, as already mentioned, choose not to take PCS assignments overseas at all. Being down range may mean you have a chance to do real work; it is highly unlikely to get you promoted.

So language skills that were already insufficient decline each year. There are periodic announcements that this will be changed and that some new incentive will be put in place to encourage officers to do the hard work necessary to really master a foreign language. Nothing much comes of them. No real advantage comes from taking the time to attend language training, and no real penalty is paid for not doing so. The problem intensifies.

All of this, of course, could not be happening at a worse time. The targets against which the DO is expected to work are getting more difficult all the time, and the price of getting an op wrong is rising. We are no longer recruiting sympathetic members of an allied nation to work against a common Communist threat. Now we are attempting to convince fanatical enemies of our nation and our culture to betray their compatriots and work against the terrorist group to which they belong. Where once a misstep meant a diplomatic protest and the return of an officer to Washington, now it means someone's death, maybe an asset, maybe our officer.

We cannot afford to retain the broken, dysfunctional personnel structure currently in place within the CIA. We built the OSS for a war against a brutal, relentless foe. We are currently locked in a worldwide struggle with another such enemy, and we need an organization that is hard, effective, and focused enough to confront that opponent.

CHAPTER FIVE

Political Football

Following completion of paramilitary training, I went into the tradecraft course to learn the nuts and bolts of how to function as an ops officer overseas. At this time the head of the facility where I trained was a senior case officer I will call "Captain Jack" for the purposes of this work. He was perhaps the single best leader I ever encountered in my career in the CIA.

Captain Jack had been in the agency for twenty-plus years and served in a wide variety of locations, most of them in the Third World. He was low key. He was humble. He was self-deprecating. He was also brilliant, thorough, and, when it came to ops, ruthless. He compiled a list of precepts for agency managers and leaders that I carry with me to this day. Let me share a portion of it with you to give you a flavor of the man:

> *Always stand up for your people. Take the blame when things go wrong, and give them the credit when things go right.*
>
> *Lead by example. Do not be a hypocrite, and never have one standard for yourself and another for others. Never ask anyone to do anything you would not do yourself.*
>
> *Remember that humility is an indispensable quality in a leader, particularly in a profession where one can go from hero to goat in a nanosecond.*
>
> *Take your work seriously but not yourself. If you are on the way up, never forget that it is the hard work and*

dedication of your colleagues that is largely responsible for your success.

You get the idea. Captain Jack was a leader. He was precisely what an organization like the CIA, one with so few gifted leaders, needed.

While in the field, Captain Jack had served in a wide variety of locales. During one tour he was in a U.S. embassy that was literally overrun by an angry mob that broke through all defenses and threatened to capture the American employees on the compound. It was Captain Jack who maintained a cool head throughout the entire affair and successfully argued against the use of lethal force in defending the embassy because he believed it would mean unnecessary loss of life and only inflame an already poisonous atmosphere. It was also Captain Jack who had planned ahead for the escape of the personnel on the compound and led them all to safety, thereby preventing harm to any of them.

Captain Jack's assignment as chief of the training facility in question was an interim assignment. Prior to arriving there, his last posting had been as chief of station. He was expected in the near future to take another post as chief, this time to an even bigger office.

Captain Jack never got that assignment. Among his many assignments had been several in Central America, and he was caught up in the firestorm that raged in the early and mid-1990s regarding CIA involvement there. He was forced to retire shortly thereafter.

In March of 1995 the president of the United States directed the Intelligence Oversight Board (IOB) to conduct a government-wide review concerning allegations regarding the 1990 death of U.S. citizen Michael DeVine, the 1992 disappearance of Guatemalan guerrilla leader Efrain Bamaca Velasquez, and related matters.[39] The scope of the inquiry covered any existing intelligence bearing on the torture, disappearance, or death of U.S. citizens in Guatemala since 1984, including not only the cases identified above but a number of other cases as well. The board also reviewed the overall U.S. intelligence relationship with Guatemala, the coordination of intelligence and policy, and the asset validation process.

The president's action in directing the IOB to conduct this review was prompted in large measure by the actions of Senator Robert Torricelli. Torricelli was known for a rather theatrical approach to public service and had already made a series of controversial unauthorized disclosures of classified information to the press. Torricelli wrote a letter to President Bill Clinton regarding the alleged killings of DeVine and Velasquez by Guatemalan forces. In that letter he charged that the Central Intelligence Agency was complicit in these murders, saying, "The direct involvement of the Central Intelligence Agency in the murder of these individuals leads me to the extraordinary conclusion that the agency is simply out of control and that it contains what can only be called a criminal element."[40]

Torricelli went on to say that "there were no U.S. security concerns in Guatemala that justified a CIA presence there. . . . This is the single worst example of the intelligence community being beyond civilian control and operating against our national interest." Torricelli identified the man responsible for the killings as a Guatemalan military intelligence officer, Colonel Julio Roberto Alpirez. Torricelli also stated that at the time of the deaths Colonel Alpirez was a "contract employee of the CIA."[41] This was apparently intended to mean that Alpirez was on the payroll of the CIA at the time as a clandestine asset.

Torricelli was not just saying that the CIA had done something wrong or advocating a change in policy. He was saying quite clearly that the CIA was "off the reservation," that it was taking actions without any authorization from the president or the Congress and that its officers were directly complicit in the murder of innocent civilians. It would be difficult to imagine more serious allegations, and one would be excused, I think, for assuming that before a United States senator would make such allegations he would be sure of his facts.

The IOB, which the president appointed, received reports from the inspectors general of the Departments of State and Justice and the CIA, and from the inspector general and general counsel of the Department of Defense. These reports covered those agencies and their subordinate agencies, such as the National Security Agency (NSA), the Defense Intelligence

Agency (DIA), the Drug Enforcement Administration (DEA), and the Federal Bureau of Investigation (FBI). The IOB also conducted its own inquiry and interviewed scores of witnesses in the United States and Guatemala and examined many thousands of documents. The board also requested a CIA IG review of all clandestine assets in Guatemala since 1984 for allegations of human rights abuse.[42]

In the end the IOB reached a number of conclusions, which I have quoted in part below. The report itself is of substantial length, and presenting it in its entirety is well beyond the scope of this work. I encourage anyone interested in the subject to read the full report. It is readily available online.

With regard to the allegation that the CIA was operating in a rogue fashion and engaging in criminal behavior, the board found that

> *. . . the intelligence community carried out activities in support of US policy objectives. These objectives included supporting the transition to and strengthening of civilian democratic government in Guatemala, encouraging respect for human rights, combating illegal narcotics trafficking, fighting the communist insurgency, and, in recent years, advancing the peace process.*

The board found that in pursuit of these objectives the CIA had an established liaison relationship with Guatemalan security services and that this relationship was known to the National Security Council, the State Department, and the Congressional oversight committees.[43]

The board stated further,

> *We found no evidence that Guatemala station was a "rogue" station operating independently of control by its headquarters. Rather, the station generally kept CIA's Directorate of Operations (DO) headquarters well-informed of all developments, negative or otherwise, including allegations against assets as they surfaced.*[44]

With regard to claims that CIA assets may have been involved in human rights violations, the board found that while it was possible violations had occurred there was no evidence whatsoever that any such actions had been taken at the direction of the CIA or as part of any CIA operation. In pondering the difficult question of when doing business with characters with histories of unsavory behavior was in the national interest, the board recommended that

> *US intelligence agencies should, while maintaining the ability to use key assets with such histories when national interests warrant, establish clear guidance on the recruitment and retention of assets with human rights or criminal allegations.*[45]

The board also found that the CIA had, by the time the report was issued, already issued such guidance.

Regarding the accusation that Alpirez had killed DeVine, the board had this to say:

> *The widely publicized allegation that Guatemalan Colonel Alpirez directed or was present at the murder of US citizen Michael DeVine appears to have been based upon information that was unreliable and was contradicted by other evidence. Numerous other reports also contradict the subsequent allegation that Colonel Alpirez killed guerrilla leader Efrain Bamaca Velasquez or was present at his death.*

While the board did not dismiss the possibility that Velasquez had been mistreated by Alpirez during his interrogation, it went on to say that there was no indication that the CIA was aware of this during the course of its relationship with Alpirez.

The board then discussed the issue of congressional notification. In this regard they stated that Congress was not always appropriately "fully and currently" informed by the CIA, particularly concerning the death of Michael DeVine. They specifically noted, however, that it was their conclusion that CIA officials did not deliberately mislead Congress and attributed their failure to inform to the "absence of a systematic notification process and inadequate emphasis upon reporting issues by CIA management."[46]

The board also took time to consider the question of Torricelli's behavior in leaking classified information.

> *The system for collecting and disseminating intelligence information can function properly only if US executive and legislative branch officials are held accountable should they compromise or improperly handle classified information. A lack of accountability puts sources of intelligence at risk. The effect is to discourage the proper provision of information by intelligence agencies to intelligence consumers and the oversight community, and ultimately to jeopardize the ability of the United States to recruit sources and to collect intelligence in the furtherance of its national interests around the world. Ample avenues exist by which well-intentioned officials can raise grievances concerning intelligence activities—either through the executive branch to the National Security Advisor or the President, or through the Congressional oversight committees to the Congressional leadership—without publicly revealing sensitive intelligence information.*
>
> ***Recommendation:***
>
> *The executive and legislative branches should hold accountable any officials known to have compromised or improperly handled classified information.*[47]

Allow me to paraphrase and summarize the findings of the board. There was no evidence whatsoever of anything approaching CIA complicity in any of the alleged human rights abuses. There was not even any reliable evidence to show that Alpirez had carried out the killings of which he was accused. The CIA needed to do a considerably better job of disseminating information and keeping all relevant parties, including Congress, in the loop, and the CIA needed to put in place a more rigorous process of balancing the value of an asset against his involvement in illegal, not to say immoral, activities.

Oh, and lest we forget, senators and congressmen who disclosed classified information without authorization should be held accountable.

This entire investigation had been initiated on the basis of allegations by a U.S. senator that the CIA had been directly involved in murder and torture, not only of Guatemalan citizens but of U.S. citizens as well. In the end no evidence was produced to support these allegations, and claims of "criminal" behavior were not supported by any evidence at all.

It did not matter. This was now a matter of politics. A lot of people were, apparently, unhappy with the direction U.S. policy had taken in Guatemala and Central America for a number of years, and the CIA was going to be made the scapegoat for that. Quite a number of individuals on Capitol Hill had already jumped in and made clear where they stood. Senators Arlen Specter and Bob Kerrey, chairman and vice-chairman, respectively, of the Senate Select Committee on Intelligence, had publicly stated that they believed the CIA had "knowingly misled" them. [48] A large number of other prominent politicians, sensing the direction of public opinion, had also already weighed in as being against the CIA. The list included Senators William Cohen, John Glenn, and John Kerry.[49]

As a result of the controversy generated by Torricelli's accusations, at least a dozen senior CIA officers were disciplined. Two were forced to resign immediately, and most of the remainder, including Captain Jack, chose to resign rather than continue to serve in disgrace. It did not matter that there had been no finding of wrongdoing on his part or for that matter on the part of any other CIA officer. These men, many of them with long and distinguished careers in the service of their country, were sacrificed for political purposes. President Clinton opined that he found the firings "forceful and fair."[50]

These actions took place in late 1995, before the Intelligence Oversight Board had even finished its report and presented its findings to the president who had appointed it. Then the CIA scrubbed its asset base for any and all with any "human rights" issues. There was not much of a methodology employed here. Twelve senior officers had just been decapitated. The DCI himself and his executive director had directed this purge. The CIA went through its asset ranks and tossed overboard pretty much anyone and everyone who had any involvement with any activity that might cause heartburn. In some parts of the world, this was a major portion of the individuals with whom station did business.

Coinciding with these actions, the CIA put in place a new procedure for balancing the value of an asset against his or her involvement in various types of objectionable activities. Not surprisingly, given the political climate, there was little real balance to this new system. It began by establishing as a default position that operational contact with anyone deemed to have violated human rights was prohibited. It then provided that in exceptional cases permission to have contact with someone with human rights "issues" could be provided by the senior leadership of the organization in response to a specific formal request.

Twelve senior officers had just lost their jobs. The president of the United States himself had taken Torricelli's accusations so seriously that he had directed a formal investigation by the IOB. The Department of Justice was still cleaning up bits and pieces of the investigation.

How many junior officers do you think stood up in that climate and asked for permission to run as an asset a guy with a checkered past? Even assuming a few mule-headed individuals with a singular focus on mission accomplishment decided they did want to stick their heads into that meat grinder, how many chiefs of station do you think were going to support making the request? I would submit probably only those who weren't too attached to their careers.

And in the event the stars aligned and a COS did back making a formal request for permission to establish a relationship with someone who had been involved in questionable activities, what do you think the reception was back at headquarters when the message came in? How long do you think it took for someone to pick up a secure phone and ask the COS in question if he had lost his mind?

I was a midlevel officer serving on the other side of the planet from Central America in 1995, and I can tell you precisely what the impact was at my level. Any contact with anyone who had come anywhere near a human rights violation of any kind or had ever had any involvement in criminal activity was shut down. End of story. No exceptions. I remember reading the guidance that came to the field and saying to a supervisor of mine at one point that technically we could still pursue individuals with other than spotless records, but we would have to get approval from top levels of the organization. He looked at me as if I had two heads and told me no one was going to stick his neck out to support anything like that. I got the message.

Let me be clear: I don't have any doubt whatsoever that during this time frame there were individuals serving in the Guatemalan security services, and those of other Central American countries, who can best be described as thugs. I have news for you—that's not a phenomenon confined to Latin America. If you want to do business in most of the developing world, you are going to have to figure out how to handle your relationship with a great number of very unsavory characters.

I also don't find it hard to believe that there were instances where CIA officers assigned to Central America did not always do all they could do to ensure that all issues concerning human rights were documented and flagged to the attention of the correct authorities both in country and back home. When you wade around all day in a difficult, dangerous, distasteful situation, sometimes you start to go numb to it. It's a defense mechanism, and if you're not careful, one day you realize you have become so jaded that it has started to affect your judgment. It takes discipline and constant reinforcement from the top to prevent that from happening.

I think the overall political context is key here, though. Everyone who had not been asleep for the last fifty years had a very clear picture of what Guatemala was and who was in charge there. The CIA knew. The State Department knew. The White House knew. Congress certainly knew. Yet we stayed engaged there. By the time Torricelli wrote his letter to Bill Clinton, the CIA alone had been involved in Guatemala for decades.

During this span of time, under a multitude of Congresses and presidents, as control passed back and forth from Republicans to Democrats and back again, we stayed involved. At some points we applied pressure and expressed displeasure. At other points we increased support and pushed the Guatemalans to assist us in our efforts to counter Communist expansion in Central America. Nobody ever told the CIA to pull out; no one ever changed the CIA's basic mission. Nothing the CIA ever did in Central America was some sort of rogue operation or the result of some random brainstorm in Langley. It was always pursuant to direction from Washington and in support of American foreign policy.

So if in 1995 someone wanted to rethink that dynamic and propose that we take a very different approach to our Guatemalan policy, that might well have been a quite reasonable course of action. Maybe we should have stopped, reviewed the situation, and considered doing something very different. I, for one, believe that we ought to choose our battles and that it is not really a requirement that we involve ourselves in the internal affairs of every nation on the planet. We have a lot of problems at home. Maybe we ought to spend more time focusing on those.

I also think that the United States of America is unique. We are not just another nation. We are a nation founded on ideals. Democracy is our state religion. No matter how difficult and distasteful the battle we must fight to defend our nation, we cannot lose track of who we are and what we are. We cannot win the war only to find we have transformed ourselves in the process into something dark, sinister, and ugly. The fact that someone is willing to ally him- or herself with us does not automatically mean we should accept such an alliance. Maybe we should have stayed engaged with the Guatemalan government. Maybe we should not have. In making either choice, however, we should have been very conscious of the consequences and the price to be paid.

How a discussion about what our foreign policy should be morphs into a witch hunt that claims the careers of many good, experienced intelligence officers, however, is another matter. This nation desperately needs a tough, disciplined, effective human intelligence organization. You can't develop such a thing if you continue to use it as a whipping post and a political football. We found out after Vietnam what our lack of support for our armed forces did to their effectiveness. We need to apply the same lesson to the CIA. Guatemala is just an example. The spin had hardly stopped on this story when Congress moved on to the investigation of patently absurd claims that the CIA was smuggling crack into Los Angeles.

The board found no evidence to support any of Torricelli's original, lurid claims. There was no indication that CIA officers were directing torture, sanctioning murder, or covering up crimes. About the most egregious thing the board had to say was that CIA headquarters was not doing a particularly good job of keeping policy makers in Washington informed of developments on the ground.

The CIA was punished anyway. The Intelligence Oversight Board issued its report on June 28, 1996. Around the world the purging of asset ranks was already well underway, and stations everywhere were running the other way from anyone with a checkered past. It was during precisely this time frame that I was instructed to break contact with the terrorist official who had agreed to work with us. If it wasn't safe, we didn't do it.

On August 7, 1998, al-Qaeda staged simultaneous attacks against our embassies in Nairobi and Dar es Salaam. Over two hundred persons, including twelve Americans, were killed. Five thousand persons were wounded.

On October 12, 2000, the USS *Cole* was attacked. Seventeen sailors were killed and thirty-nine wounded. The vessel came perilously close to sinking. Whether we were ready to admit it or not, we were already at war.

In neither case did the CIA provide warning of the impending attacks. None of the stations involved had sources who could provide the requisite intelligence. It is, after all, very difficult to find a good source inside a terrorist organization who has a clean record when it comes to human rights. Terrorist organizations are tight, compartmentalized organizations. They do not broadcast their plans. The only individuals inside such an entity who know about planning for attacks are individuals who are to some extent involved in that planning. They are terrorists, and to get to the point of being trusted with sensitive information, they will not only have been vetted, they will have been tested.

In the wake of the fallout from the Guatemalan investigation, no COS on the planet was prepared to risk his neck by climbing into bed with someone with blood on his hands. Even if he was, no one back home in headquarters was going to support him.

"Don't fall."

"No ops. No problems."

I am not making a case here that the fallout from the Guatemalan investigation and the ensuing purge were the sole, direct cause of the CIA's failure to be positioned to head off these attacks. As should be patently obvious, I hope, by this point in this manuscript, it is my contention that the CIA is dying a death of a thousand cuts. There is no one, single cause for any of the crises it has encountered.

I will say this, however: If we are serious about having an intelligence organization that is going to be charged with penetrating dangerous, evil organizations filled with dangerous, evil men, then we need to accept that we are going to have to utilize the services of some very distasteful individuals. I have run a lot of terrorist sources over the years. None of them was someone I would bring home to meet the family.

We are also going to have to get out of this cycle of using the CIA as a political football and making attacks on the organization a form of proxy war on whatever administration is in power. We accept that the armed forces serve the people of the country. We debate foreign and defense policy vigorously. We do not attack the men and women in uniform regardless of our feelings or political leanings. We must reach the same place, mentally and emotionally, with regard to the CIA or whatever replaces it. Crippling purges and witch hunts not only destroy careers, they cost us lives. Captain Jack had to find a new job. Several hundred people in East Africa paid a far higher price.

These are not new issues. The OSS walked through this same moral and ethical minefield in its struggle against Nazi Germany. Particularly when one reads the accounts of OSS operations behind enemy lines in Greece, Albania, and Yugoslavia,[51] one finds graphic evidence of how difficult it was to maintain the balance between our core values and the necessity to find allies in a struggle against a common foe.

Fifteen German Army divisions, assisted by a hundred thousand native occupation forces, were assigned to Yugoslavia to maintain order during the Second World War. Beginning in 1943, the Allies were slogging their way northward through Italy against the determined and skillful opposition of the German forces there. It was imperative that the Germans be prevented from moving their troops in Yugoslavia out and into Italy. Accordingly, both OSS and British intelligence teams jumped into Yugoslavia to work with the partisans.[52]

What the OSS found on the ground was a tangled, vicious political situation. Resistance to the Germans on the ground was divided between Communist forces loyal to Josip Tito and Chetnik forces loyal to Draja Mihailovich. They both hated the Germans; they also hated each other at least as much.

As was typical of OSS performance throughout the war, the achievements of the teams sent into Yugoslavia were incredible. By October of 1944 there were fifteen OSS teams working with Tito's forces. They provided intelligence on a host of political and military topics, and they transmitted daily German order-of-battle reports to headquarters, including maps of locations to be bombed by Allied air. They also coordinated critical resupply operations that enabled Yugoslav forces to continue their fight against the Axis.[53] Working with local partisans, OSS officers also rescued downed Allied fliers, housed them, and flew them out to safety from secret airfields they constructed. In one operation alone, Operation Halyard, OSS officers working with Yugoslav partisans orchestrated the successful aerial extraction of 512 downed Allied airmen from inside Yugoslavia.[54] Before the war ended in Europe, almost sixteen hundred men had been rescued in this fashion. [55]

In June of 1944 one section of a team code-named ALUM successfully crossed from Yugoslavia into the Reich itself. For forty-four days, operating from a hidden bunker they constructed on a mountainside, the team transmitted intelligence on the movement of rail traffic on the key Zidani Most to Ljubljana line. This intelligence was obtained by direct observation and also through a network of local sources run by the team.[56] As a consequence the Allies were able to gain a total picture of all rail traffic moving by this critical route into both Italy and Greece.[57] This intelligence was of immense, truly strategic significance and unobtainable in any other fashion.

To get these kinds of results, OSS operatives were forced to swim through a sea of swirling, often conflicting allegiances. Team Ranger, led by Lieutenant Colonel Robert McDowell, jumped into Serbia in August 1944. On the ground McDowell married up with Chetnik forces and, while rescuing downed fliers and gathering intelligence, had an opportunity to see firsthand the ferocity of this triangular conflict. Wrote McDowell:

> *I never have had much time to interrogate Partisan prisoners because if I get to them within half an hour after capture, they are executed by knife. Prisoners are killed by both sides. All Partisans (Tito's followers), dead or wounded, are relieved of their boots, shoes and serviceable clothing immediately if they have any. . . . Hatred runs so high that I have seen men kick the dead after a battle.*[58]

McDowell was in charge of a tiny team, completely dependent on the Chetniks for security and survival and desperately trying to leverage their capabilities in the larger context of the war against Nazi Germany. He was powerless to impact their behavior or that of their adversaries.

OSS officers working with Tito's forces designed and implemented a campaign to disseminate propaganda encouraging German forces to surrender. So effective was the campaign that Tito's men were overwhelmed by the flow of prisoners with which they were faced. They had neither the facilities nor the logistics to support the housing and control of the numbers of men turning themselves in. They solved the problem by simply shooting German and satellite troops once they had put down their arms.[59] Helpless to stop the killing, OSS terminated the propaganda campaign rather than be a party to the continuing executions.[60]

In Greece the OSS found a very similar situation, with competing guerrilla organizations combating the Germans in a vicious war in which no quarter was asked and none given. The Greeks, inflamed by atrocities committed by the Nazis, responded by inflicting slow, excruciatingly painful deaths on German soldiers they captured. OSS operatives, working in small bands in the countryside with their Greek supporters, tried their utmost to control this behavior and to adhere to the laws of war. They were not always successful. In some cases OSS officers were actually forced to shoot German prisoners themselves in order to spare them from the far more painful, and protracted, agony of death by torture at the hands of enraged Greek civilians.

I don't have any easy answers for the ethical dilemmas we face in attempting to run intelligence operations and conduct covert action. I certainly do not advocate that we condone execution or mistreatment of prisoners. As I noted above, we are fighting, in any war, for the preservation of the United States of America. That means more than just defending its territorial integrity—that also means preserving all those ideals that define us as a nation.

What I do know, though, is that it is critical that we succeed in finding a way to run the kinds of operations that are required for victory. We cannot afford not to. The ongoing war on terror will be fought far more by intelligence operatives and special forces than it will be by armored divisions and strategic bombers. All the massed conventional troops on the planet are not going to help us root out al-Qaeda cells in the Middle East or interdict radiological material on its way from the former Soviet Union to the tribal areas of Pakistan.

To do this we are going to have to work together. The CIA, or its successor, has to be treated as a national asset and supported as such. Clearly, its actions need to be in accordance with national policy and pursuant to the direction and control of the president and the Congress. The CIA is not some sort of private club. It is a tool, owned and paid for by the taxpayers of the United States. That said, when the CIA takes action as directed, Congress needs to stand behind it and support it. Without that support and the confidence it will inspire, no human intelligence organization has a prayer of accomplishing the things we must require of it.

CHAPTER SIX

The Legion

It's hard to know whether to laugh or cry in talking about the Iran-Contra Affair. Should we be outraged by the blatant disregard by the officials of the Reagan administration for the Constitution and the Congress of the United States? Or should we simply be overcome by the depths of their grotesque incompetence? These were men who claimed to be on the cutting edge of covert operations, and yet from the outset they bungled virtually every aspect of this endeavor.

The history of the Iran-Contra Affair begins with the overthrow of the Somoza government in Nicaragua in 1979 and the rise to power of the Communist Sandinistas. In response to this development, Ronald Reagan directed the CIA to begin a secret effort to arm, train, and equip forces opposed to the Sandinistas. These forces, led principally by former military officers from the Somoza regime, became known as the Contras.

In response to these actions, on December 8, 1982, Congress passed a bill prohibiting U.S. covert actions "for the purpose of overthrowing the government of Nicaragua" but allowing some limited continued funding for the Contras. This action was prompted at least in part by reports that the Contras were attacking soft targets not of a military nature and by concern about civilian casualties from their operations.

In May 1984 Congress discovered that despite the 1982 restrictions, the Reagan administration was continuing to support the Contras and to undertake actions directly against the government of Nicaragua. Among other things Congress determined that the CIA, acting under the direction of National Security Council member Oliver North, was mining Nicaraguan harbors. Consequently, Congress cut off all funding for the Contras and passed the Boland Amendment, a statute prohibiting any U.S. agency involved in "intelligence activities" from "supporting, directly or indirectly, military or paramilitary operations in Nicaragua by any nation, group, organization or individual."

This guidance would seem clear enough, but apparently, it was not clear enough for the Reagan administration. In fact, both direct and indirect support for the Contras continued despite the Boland Amendment. Coordinated by Oliver North via a series of activities he dubbed the "Enterprise," money and arms for the Contras were obtained from countries such as South Africa, Brunei, South Korea, Israel, and Saudi Arabia; from wealthy Americans supportive of the Contras; and from arms sales to Iran. Money earned from sales of weaponry to Iran was diverted into secret channels to support Contra activities.

This continued for roughly two years. Then on October 5, 1986, Nicaraguan government soldiers shot down an American cargo plane that was carrying military supplies to Contra forces. The lone surviving crew member, American Eugene Hasenfus, was taken into captivity and confessed that he was employed by the CIA. A month after Hasenfus was shot down, on November 3, 1986, President Reagan's secret sale of U.S. arms to Iran was reported by a Lebanese publication. Not long thereafter, on November 25, 1986, Attorney General Edwin Meese announced that Justice Department officials had discovered that some of the proceeds from the Iran arms sales had been diverted to the Contras.

Congressional hearings ensued, and in December 1986 Lawrence E. Walsh was appointed independent counsel by the U.S. Court of Appeals for the District of Columbia Circuit. Reagan administration officials, not content with having deliberately circumvented the will of Congress, then began what can only be described as a concerted effort to impede the investigation. In the words of Walsh's final report,

> *Following the revelation of [the Iran-Contra] operations in October and November 1986, Reagan Administration officials deliberately deceived the Congress and the public about the level and extent of official knowledge of and support for these operations.*[61]

The investigation lasted from 1986 to 1994. Ultimately, Walsh charged a total of fourteen Reagan administration officials with criminal acts. Eleven of these individuals were either convicted or pleaded guilty to federal crimes. Several individuals, including Secretary of Defense Caspar Weinberger, were issued pretrial pardons by President George H. W. Bush during the lame-duck period following his electoral defeat in 1992. Walsh concluded that "the sales of arms to Iran contravened United States Government policy and may have violated the Arms Export Control Act," that "the provision and coordination of support to the Contras violated the Boland Amendment ban on aid to military activities in Nicaragua," and that "the Iran operations were carried out with the knowledge of, among others, President Ronald Reagan, Vice President George H. W. Bush, Secretary of State George P. Schultz, Secretary of Defense Caspar W. Weinberg, and Director of Central Intelligence William J. Casey."[62]

What was clear at the time and has remained clear ever since was that this was not a case of a rogue operation. Despite efforts in the cover-up to designate certain individuals as scapegoats and to limit the amount of information that was released regarding the scope of the operation, it became obvious early on that the Enterprise was the product of a deliberate decision by the executive branch to simply disregard the authority of the Congress of the United States and to finance and conduct a war abroad based purely on its own discretion.

What remained less clear and has, due to issues of classification of sensitive data, remained so to this day was the degree of CIA complicity in the entire affair. That said, what did come out in the course of the investigation by the independent counsel showed that, at least at the senior levels, a significant number of CIA officers were not only aware of the activities of the Enterprise but also deliberately directed that the agency "dovetail" its operations on the ground in Central America with those of North and his cohorts.[63] What also became clear was that once the investigation began these same officials chose to attempt to impede the efforts of the independent counsel and Congress and repeatedly lied under oath.

Director Casey's support for President Reagan's Contra policies and for the Iran arms sales was crucial in this regard. Casey was directly involved in putting Oliver North together with retired General Secord, who was a key part of the conspiracy. He did this subsequent to the passage of the Boland Amendment and in direct response to the impact of that legislation on the CIA's efforts to aid the Contras. He also supported Secord's involvement in the Iranian arms sales, despite the fact that there were significant numbers of individuals within the CIA who had deep reservations about Secord and several of his partners in this endeavor. Throughout the course of the two years that the Enterprise was functioning, Casey also met on a regular basis with North, and it appears clear that he personally provided a great deal of operational guidance to North. Casey also was directly involved in the details of synchronizing CIA operations with those of North, often bypassing normal CIA channels in the process.

Four CIA officials were eventually charged with criminal offenses: Clair George, the deputy director for operations and the third-highest-ranking CIA official; Dewey Clarridge, chief of the European Division; Alan Fiers, chief of the Central American Task Force; and Joseph Fernandez, Costa Rican station chief. George was convicted of two felony counts of false statements and perjury before Congress. Fiers pleaded guilty to two misdemeanor counts of withholding information from Congress. The four counts of obstruction and false statements against Fernandez were dismissed when the Bush administration refused to declassify information needed for his defense. Clarridge was awaiting trial on seven counts of perjury and false statements when he, George, and Fiers were pardoned by President Bush. In the course of the investigation, Fiers conceded that he had lied to Congress, justifying his actions by saying that he did so to "keep the spotlight off the White House."[64]

Casey himself suffered a seizure in his office on December 15, 1986, and died on May 6, 1987. Independent Counsel never questioned him, and only a few notes of his concerning the matter were ever recovered.

The Iran-Contra Affair was not simply a CIA operation. It was much larger than that, and in some respects the CIA played a bit part. That said, ultimately, it proved to be a debacle of epic proportions for the organization. Pardons and legal technicalities aside, five of the top officers in the organization, including the director and the chief of the Directorate of Operations, had been exposed as having committed federal crimes. No one went to jail, but the careers of four of the five ended in disgrace. Casey escaped the same fate only by virtue of a premature death.

As disastrous as the affair was and as inexcusable as the actions of senior officers were in attempting to stonewall a legal inquiry and circumvent the will of Congress, however, it is important that we focus on how this entire project was started and who was behind it. This was not a CIA operation. CIA officers sitting in Langley did not come up with a bright idea one day to bypass the clear intent of the Boland Amendment, sell arms to the Iranians, and establish a secret funding mechanism for the Contras. The White House and the National Security Council did that.

Having made the decision to disregard the authority of Congress and having presumed—based on what constitutional interpretation remains unclear—that it could do pretty much anything it wanted outside the borders of the United States on its own authority, the White House assumed from the outset that it also could direct the Central Intelligence Agency to cooperate pretty much as it chose. In other words, from the optic of the White House, the CIA apparently did not work for Congress or the American people; it worked solely for the executive branch.

That, I think, is a critical point and is at the heart of what has so damaged the standing of the CIA in the last few decades. It has come to be viewed by the president of the United States not as a national asset but as his personal possession. Employment of the CIA is not dependent on Congressional support or the backing of the American people. The CIA, apparently, does the bidding of the president, even when it is clear that his desires run completely contrary to those of the people's representatives on the Hill.

There is a larger context here, a full exploration of which is well beyond the scope of this book. This same attitude on the part of presidents may, in fact, have come to apply to large elements of foreign and defense policy in general. Increasingly, it seems that presidents believe they have some sort of unilateral authority, not simply to respond to time-sensitive military crises but to make all the decisions regarding America's foreign entanglements in general.

I have no illusions about the efficiency of the Congress of the United States. It is a large, ungainly machine. Some of its members are statesmen and intellects of the first order. Some of its members are significantly less impressive. It works slowly and reluctantly, and sometimes we all just want to cry in frustration at the difficulty it has in recognizing what needs to be done.

It is important, however, that we remember one key fact: It works exactly the way it was designed to work. In fact, the comments above regarding the Congress probably apply to the United States government as a whole: It too works exactly as it was meant to—slowly, cautiously, inefficiently, reluctantly.

The Founding Fathers were not idiots. They knew how to build a much more effective and efficient government. In fact, they had direct experience with such a structure: It was called a monarchy. They knew very well that a king could make decisions much more quickly and decisively than any body of hundreds of men. They also knew very well that splitting that legislative body in two and then making it share power with an executive branch and the judiciary was just going to add to the difficulty of deciding on a course of action.

The Founders also knew the price that was paid for the efficiency and rapidity of action that came with a monarchy. A king could react to a foreign crisis immediately and direct an appropriate military response. In the process he might also get the entire nation into a war, which might or might not enjoy the support of all those thousands of individuals who would actually be called upon to fight it. The Founding Fathers were willing to give up a little efficiency in the interest of ensuring that the nation did not get involved in conflicts and entanglements abroad unless its duly elected representatives were supportive.

The Constitution of the United States does not go into tremendous detail regarding exactly how authority in the conduct of foreign affairs and national defense is to be divided. What it does say, however, clearly contemplates a sharing of power. The president is the commander in chief. Congress has the sole power to declare war, and the Senate must ratify treaties. What all this means in any given situation is the subject of much debate among legal and constitutional scholars. What is readily apparent, however, is that nothing in the Constitution suggests even vaguely that the president has some sort of unilateral authority to simply conduct foreign affairs as he sees fit. Somehow, some way, that task has to be shared between the legislative and executive branches under the watchful eye of the judiciary.

When the Reagan administration took the steps it did to create the Enterprise, it acted in direct contravention of that fact. There was no question whatsoever as to where the Congress of the United States stood on the issue of the Contras. Over a period of years, Congress had made crystal clear that it did not want the government of the United States involved in supporting the Contras and that it did not stand behind any action to overthrow the Sandinista government of Nicaragua. The Reagan administration acted anyway, and without any apparent hesitation, it ordered the CIA to assist.

The reason the CIA was chosen, of course, and not, say, the Federal Highway Administration, is that the CIA is designed to work quietly and surreptitiously. It has all the right tools to carry out an operation of this kind without detection. There's only one problem: Those capabilities exist to conceal CIA operations from our enemies. They do not exist so that we can hide CIA operations from the elected representatives of the people.

The CIA does not belong to the president of the United States any more than the United States Navy belongs to him. He may be the commander in chief, but he is not a king. He does not own the armed services, the FBI, the CIA, or any of the other elements of the federal government. He has significant authority to direct their actions, but they are not his possessions.

When the executive branch chooses to act as if the CIA somehow belongs exclusively to it, the result is corrosive and destructive. I discussed in the previous chapter the desperate necessity for the CIA to have the full support of the Congress and the American people if we are to expect it to take the kind of risky, aggressive operations we so desperately need. That kind of support is impossible as long as the president continues to think of the CIA as his personal asset and to employ it in situations where there is no broad foundation of political support.

I am not suggesting that the CIA, or a new OSS, only be used in situations where some sort of "declaration of war" has been passed. By definition the CIA is meant to be used in those kinds of situations where we are not prepared to initiate full-blown, overt hostilities. That said, I do think it is key, particularly when we are talking about covert action as opposed to normal intelligence collection, that a new OSS be employed only in situations wherein it is clear that the president and the majority of the Congress agree that action needs to be taken. At a minimum, I think we could say quite confidently that a new OSS should never be used in an operation the transparent purpose of which is to circumvent the will of the legislature.

On February 25, 1945, two OSS operatives and one Austrian deserter who had been recruited as an agent jumped into the Tyrol region of West Austria.[65] With the assistance of cooperative Austrian contacts on the ground, the team then set up operations in the mountains and established radio communications with their headquarters. Over the next several weeks, they began to disseminate intelligence gained from a network of human sources and from local resistance organizations. They gained intelligence on Nazi plans for resistance in the Alpine areas of southern Germany; located two aircraft plants; and provided detailed reports on the movements of Mussolini, the establishment of Himmler's new headquarters, and other topics.

One of the two OSS operatives was an American army sergeant named Frederick Mayer. Mayer was born in Germany. He was also a Jew.[66] He spent a large portion of the time he was on the ground in Oberpfuss, a suburb of Innsbruck, and utilized the uniform of a German army officer and false documents to move around freely and to maintain contact with a network of anti-Nazis, who gave him details of train schedules, freight and troop movements, and factory production. All of this information was sent by radio to OSS in Italy.[67]

Mayer was eventually identified and arrested when an agent of his, a black marketeer, was pulled in on unrelated charges. Desperate to help himself, the agent offered up information on Mayer to the Gestapo. Mayer, refusing to cooperate when questioned, was beaten for hours, until his face became a bloody pulp and one of his eardrums ruptured. Only when confronted by his own agent did Mayer concede he was an American operative. Even then, however, he refused to provide any information of value to his German interrogators.[68]

The beatings continued for days. Mayer was stripped and forced to sit on the bare floor. He was hung upside down by his handcuffed arms from the ceiling. Water was forced into his nose and ears, and he was bullwhipped.

Mayer gave up nothing. He was ultimately dumped naked on a bed of straw in a cell with his arms still chained behind his back. Lying there, he listened as a prisoner in the next cell was literally tortured to death. It seemed it was only a matter of time until he met the same fate.[69]

Around Mayer, however, the events of the larger war were unfolding, and they were not going unnoticed by the Nazis. Mayer was brought from his cell to a meeting with senior Nazi officials in Innsbruck. Incredibly, they informed Mayer that they were willing to discuss the surrender of the city of Innsbruck to Allied forces and allowed Mayer to communicate this offer to OSS headquarters. Then over the next few days they continued to meet with Mayer, ultimately agreeing not only to surrender the city and all German forces in it to him but also allowing themselves to be put under house arrest by him.

On May 3, 1945, the 103rd Infantry Division of the United States Army approached the western boundaries of the city of Innsbruck with orders to seize the city. Within the city remained heavily armed German units. Major resistance was expected; significant casualties were anticipated.

The American forces, however, were met not by German panzers but by a car containing two German soldiers waving a white flag made from a bedsheet and driven by Mayer. Mayer exited the vehicle, spoke for a period of time with the division intelligence officer, and advised that not only Innsbruck but the entire province had surrendered and he was prepared to take officers from the 103rd to meet with the necessary German authorities to effect the transfer of control.[70] The Germans had surrendered to a Jewish NCO named Mayer.

That's another one of those great OSS stories. It reminds us of the incredible courage and resolve of the men and women of that organization. Simply the fact that a Jew born and raised in Germany would agree to put on a uniform and jump back into the heart of the Third Reich is almost unbelievable. That he would survive the Gestapo and force the surrender of an entire city is truly magnificent.

I have cited the story here, though, to illustrate another point as well. Mayer, alone and in Gestapo custody, was able by virtue of his willpower, courage, and presence of mind to pull off one of the great coups of the Second World War. Singlehandedly, acting as a representative of the United States government, he negotiated and accepted the surrender of tens of thousands of German soldiers, a major city, and the surrounding province.

Mayer was able to do this, however, only because of the nature of the conflict in which he was involved and the fact that he had the full, united authority of the United States government behind him. He was a participant in a declared war, with the secure knowledge that the president, the Congress, and the American people supported him. When the Nazi governors of Innsbruck offered to exchange roles and become his prisoners, he did not have to hesitate and wonder about the boundaries of his authority or explaining his actions. He did not have to mull over his exact legal status or be concerned because he was fighting in an undeclared and secret war. He was standing on a stable, secure platform and knew his actions would be supported.

It has become a rare occasion when we have offered our clandestine operatives and intelligence officers this kind of support and backing. More typically in recent years, we have placed them in situations where they are expected to perform miracles but hung out to dry when things do not work out the way we want them. Presidents, in particular, have made a habit of tasking the

CIA to take actions that are not supported by the country as a whole and do not even enjoy the support of a simple majority in the Congress.

The results, as we have seen, can be catastrophic. If we want an OSS that can accomplish what the original did, if we want officers to take the same kind of bold, decisive, lifesaving actions that Mayer did, then we need to provide the necessary political foundation for their work. Either be prepared to support them or don't send them. "Disavowing their actions" makes for a great line in a movie. It does not work nearly as well in practice.

CHAPTER SEVEN

Everybody into the Pool

IMAGINE, IF YOU WILL, A SERIES OF DISASTERS INVOLVING NAVAL aviation. An F-18 crashes on landing on a carrier in the Atlantic. A helicopter free-falls into the sea shortly after takeoff from a carrier in the Persian Gulf. Two jets collide during an exercise in California, killing both pilots. A fire breaks out below decks on a carrier in the Pacific, and the ship almost sinks before the flames are brought under control. A naval air-strike force going after a terrorist chemical warfare complex in the Middle East experiences unexpectedly heavy losses from air defenses and fails to destroy its target.

Now imagine what the reaction might be. The events would doubtless get a lot of attention. Press coverage would be intense. Politicians on Capitol Hill would call for inquiries. Commentators would express the usual wide variety of opinions as to the cause of the sudden spate of accidents and failures. Perhaps a commission would be appointed to look into the entire issue.

In time conclusions would be reached. It might be determined that training standards had slackened, that maintenance funds had been cut, that aging airframes had been pushed beyond their operational life cycles. Any number of corrective measures might be introduced: new training courses, inspections of all aircraft in the fleet, new flight operations procedures, and so on.

Almost certainly, however, we can say that one solution to the problems encountered would *not* be to instruct the Central

Intelligence Agency to begin to build, man, equip, and operate nuclear aircraft carriers.

No matter what problems the United States Navy might be encountering in dealing with naval flight operations, no one with any common sense would think it would be a good idea to take an organization like the CIA, with no experience in flight operations at sea, and ask it to begin to take over the navy's job. We might well make the navy buckle down, tighten its standards, and clean up its act. We would certainly not ask another organization to begin to try to duplicate the incredible expertise of the U.S. Navy in this field, compiled as it has been over many decades of operations in peace and war.

Yet remarkably, since 9/11 this is exactly the approach that we have begun to take with regard to intelligence operations. Having established that the CIA is not producing the intelligence we need, rather than concentrating on fixing it or replacing it with an organization that will get the job done, we have decided to begin to allow a host of other less capable organizations to duplicate the CIA's activities.

In any given locale abroad, therefore, at the present time, you may have half a dozen or more U.S. intelligence and law enforcement entities all attempting to run their own strategic intelligence operations on top of, around, and through ongoing CIA intelligence activity. These organizations include not only the Defense HUMINT Service (DH), which was created to run clandestine operations against targets overseas, but also entities like the Naval Criminal Investigative Service (NCIS) and the Air Force Office of Special Investigations (AFOSI). The latter two are organizations that traditionally have run criminal investigations and focused on counterintelligence (CI). They were not built to run collection operations abroad focused on foreign targets. To the extent there is a traffic cop at all in this mess, it is the CIA chief of station, but his authority is under increasing attack, and his direction is more and more likely to be taken as advisory rather than compulsory.

I went out to be COS in a Middle Eastern nation several years ago, shortly after my predecessor and the head of the local NCIS office in that country had gotten into an epic head-butting competition. The NCIS chief had informed the COS that he was going to run collection operations of his own in the country in question. In short, he was going to have his personnel begin to recruit spies. He would keep the CIA informed, and he would coordinate to the extent he could. He was not, however, asking permission; he was moving forward no matter what the CIA thought.

My predecessor was livid. He threatened dire consequences. He fired off messages. He waited for the fire and brimstone and retribution. Nothing happened.

About that time I was processing out of headquarters and getting ready to get on a plane to head out for my new assignment. I was called into the front office of NE Division and given clear direction by my immediate superior. I was to take over as COS, I was to patch things up with NCIS, and I was to make the whole problem go away. There would be no headquarters support. No one in the CIA was really sure anymore that they had the authority to tell NCIS what to do. I was, in short, working without a net. If an op by any agency went wrong in country on my watch, I would probably be hung, but I was not really armed with the authority to control anyone other than my own people.

As should be readily apparent by this point in the narrative, I am no apologist for the CIA. My central thesis is, after all, that the CIA needs to be replaced, as it is incapable of doing the job for which it was created. That said, whatever the level at which the CIA is performing presently in its core mission of the collection of strategic level foreign intelligence (FI), it is significantly above that of the organizations, mostly military, that are currently imposing themselves on its turf.

Part of the issue is personnel. I have known military case officers who were superb, but on average, when it comes to the running of strategic-level intelligence operations, there is no comparison between the quality of CIA case officers and those individuals who are qualified as operations officers and serving inside NCIS, AFOSI, and others. The CIA has the cream of the crop, period. This is not arrogance. Like most things it is a function of the way the system is designed. The CIA goes out and recruits case officers to perform that specific task. As I have stated earlier, the CIA does a fairly poor job of finding leaders, but it does a very good job of finding and bringing on board individuals who can recruit spies and run operations.

The military services do not recruit case officers as such. They recruit officers and enlisted personnel to perform a host of other tasks, and then they try to take some of those individuals and essentially convert them into case officers. Occasionally, they have brilliant success. More commonly, they end up with individuals who are bright, motivated, and hardworking but who simply do not have the natural skills that CIA ops officers have.

There is also, quite frankly, no comparison in experience level. The average CIA case officer is going to run more operations and make more recruitments in a single tour than his military counterpart will in his entire career. However fast the CIA is moving, and it is clearly not fast enough, it is at light speed compared to the other organizations now trying to play on the same field. The CIA case officer is also going to spend his career running agents, whereas his military counterpart is quite likely to spend at most a few years out of his entire career involved in this activity. As is true with most professions, there is only so much you can learn in training. The real education begins once you are in the field, and there is simply no substitute for repetition and exposure to actual operations.

Part of the reason is structural. DH was built to run offensive intelligence operations abroad involving the recruitment of foreign spies. That makes it an exception among the various military services I have discussed. To the extent that organizations like NCIS have been involved in intelligence operations in the past, they have been limited to the running of double agents, usually American citizens, against foreign intelligence services. This is important and difficult work, but it is an entirely different business from attempting to penetrate a terrorist organization or take apart a nuclear proliferation network. A machine built to perform CI work is not by any means automatically capable of collecting FI and running foreign assets.

That said, the biggest issue regarding military HUMINT operations has to do with bureaucracy and command structure. Today's CIA, as risk averse and tentative as it has become, is still an infinitely more flexible and agile organization than anything that exists within military channels. While the military is thinking about putting together a proposal for an operation to be briefed to the secretary of defense for his approval, the CIA will have already initiated and concluded the operation. Particularly in today's world, in the struggle against terror, speed is everything. If you cannot move now, there is no point in moving at all. The enemy who is currently exposed and vulnerable will no longer be so by the time you finish your PowerPoint presentations and multiple video teleconferences.

I was involved several years ago in an operation directed at the capture of an al-Qaeda operative. In brief the plan for this operation involved having assets of ours bag the target and bring him to a location where he would be handed over to us. It was unclear whether our assets could pull off the snatch, but there appeared to be nothing to lose either, so we decided to move ahead.

On board in the location in question, I had a handful of officers and a quantity of firearms. I believed I could pull off the operation, but I was also aware that, as in most such situations, there was a significant chance it might be a setup. We might show up to take possession of the target and find we were the ones being served up for an ambush.

Nearby was a major U.S. military presence. Included in that presence were military intelligence and special operations types. I made the decision to approach them and request their assistance. They had the ability to supplement our capabilities significantly.

The first couple of conversations went well. The guys I was talking to were friends whom I knew well. We socialized regularly, and I had bought them any number of beers. We seemed well on our way to getting an op off the ground in short order.

Then I showed up for the third meeting, the one at which we were really going to hammer out details and a timetable. I walked into the office where we had met the first two times, and I was told by a clerk that the meeting had been moved into the auditorium down the hall. Confused, I walked down the hall of the military command's headquarters building and into the auditorium.

I was expecting to see the handful of individuals with whom I had met before. They were there, but so were seventy-plus other individuals. Someone was showing a PowerPoint presentation on a large screen in the front of the room. I was directed to a seat and then spent the better part of the next hour listening to individuals I did not know discuss the details of the impending operation. The meeting ended without any concrete decisions on any subject. I learned that there would be another planning session in a week, after which a briefing was planned for the general officer in charge of the area of operations.

I left the room stunned. One of my prime contacts in the military command in question pulled me aside in the hallway and told me that he had just been informed that a general officer at a location a thousand miles away was now going to assume direct tactical control of the actual rendezvous with the asset who would be bringing the captured al-Qaeda leader to us. Based on information that would be relayed to him, this general officer would then decide whether to proceed with taking custody of the prisoner and give instructions to us via radio.

I pulled the plug. I reminded my contact that this was a CIA operation and the military was supporting. I was not going to take direction from a general officer in a command center a thousand miles away about whether to trust my own asset. I was going to make the call on what to do at the rendezvous based on my knowledge of the individuals involved; my sense of the overall situation; and, ultimately, my gut. There was no way any of that was going to translate to a command post in a remote location. I walked away. That night I gave the green light for the operation to proceed, and things were put in motion.

Ultimately, the op failed, not because of anything to do with what was discussed above but simply because the assets on the ground where the target was located botched the snatch and were captured. Nothing ventured, nothing gained. We moved on to new targets and the search for new ways to get at the senior al-Qaeda individuals we were hunting.

My point herein is that the kind of procedures employed by the U.S. military in this case are representative of the way in which that large, complex, often cumbersome organizational structure approaches operations in general. It may work well for conventional operations, although I have my doubts in that regard as well. It is completely unsuited for intelligence operations and the kind of small-scale, fast-moving covert operations associated with them. In the world of intelligence, particularly when it comes to counterterrorism, decisions need to be made at the lowest possible level, and they need to be made now.

I have watched military case officers assigned to DH spend nine months to a year attempting to get approval to initiate human and technical operations that would have been concluded from start to finish by their CIA counterparts in less than half that time. I once saw an officer assigned to DH send off a message requesting permission to recruit a source and receive back from his headquarters an eighty-nine-page message asking for additional information on subjects so obscure and insignificant as to rival the debate over how many angels can dance on the head of a pin. Operations that would have been approved within the CIA at the level of a junior desk officer were put on hold, because it was necessary to obtain the personal signature of the Secretary of Defense in order for a DH case officer to move.

This was in most cases not a reflection on the quality of the military case officers involved. It was a product of the incredible bureaucratic inertia generated by an organizational structure that required that every decision be scrutinized by seemingly endless layers of bureaucracy and that required permission in advance for even the smallest steps. While CIA case officers were writing two-page messages detailing actions already taken, their military counterparts were drafting eighty-page submissions requesting permission to do something.

One of the horrible side effects of the refusal of senior CIA leadership to admit the full scope of the internal problems besetting that organization is that many other elements of the defense and intelligence communities have simply decided to write off the CIA and move ahead with the development of their own duplicate capabilities. Within the Department of Defense, in particular, there is a massive effort underway to stand up elements that are, on paper at least, able to perform all the tasks for which the CIA was designed. Where the director of National Intelligence stands on all this is, to me at least, unclear, but the fact remains that it is happening. If the military cannot rely upon the CIA to provide the intel they need, they will create a machine capable of getting it for them and end their reliance on the CIA entirely.

Leaving aside the horrible inefficiency of all this from a fiscal standpoint and the fact that American taxpayers are already overtaxed paying for a massive federal government, this is, from an operational perspective, an absolutely horrible idea. We will end up when this is all done with a huge, well-trained, and well-equipped military HUMINT intelligence apparatus that will be completely incapable of moving with the speed, flexibility, and subtlety necessary to conduct intelligence operations.

I mentioned earlier the actions of Gary Schroen and those individuals who went with him into Afghanistan and constituted the first American team to enter that country in the days following September 11, 2001. That team consisted entirely of CIA officers; there were no military personnel assigned. This was not because the CIA did not want to include military personnel; it was because the Department of Defense refused to make these individuals available.

In the days leading up to the departure of Schroen's team from the United States for insertion into Afghanistan, numerous efforts were made to convince the U.S. military to add at least a limited number of military personnel to Schroen's team. Not surprisingly, all the contacts with working-level individuals in Delta Force, Special Operations Command, and Central Command produced enthusiastic responses. There was no shortage of highly trained special operations personnel on the military side of the house who were dying for the opportunity to suit up and get into the fight.[71] The reaction of the establishment within the Department of Defense was quite different.

No one in the military could provide a clear response as to what military forces would and would not be introduced into Afghanistan. There was an ongoing debate over what the military's mission should be. No one had decided where and when to position air assets, and as things stood there was no search-and-rescue capability to provide for the extraction of soldiers if they were wounded or became ill. The Department of Defense was reluctant to introduce personnel on the ground without having this capability. It appeared that for the time being it was just too dangerous to send U.S. military personnel into Afghanistan.[72]

So a small team of CIA officers, riding in an antiquated Russian helicopter acquired for the mission, made the insertion while thousands of highly trained men and women in the Special Operations community of the U.S. military stood by and watched.

The problems with the Department of Defense did not end with the arrival of Schroen's team in country. On October 3, 2001, he wrote the first of three field-appraisal messages from Afghanistan in an attempt to spur the U.S. military into taking action. Bombing attacks on the Taliban had still not begun, because no infrastructure was in place to rescue downed pilots.[73] The official word coming from headquarters was that the Department of Defense had yet to reach an agreement on what forces should be introduced and when. Meanwhile, the Afghans supporting the CIA team on the ground continued daily to demand an explanation as to when military assets would be deployed.

On October 10, 2001, Schroen received a call from CIA headquarters advising him that the logjam regarding deployment of military special operations personnel remained unbroken and suggesting that it was now his responsibility to break it. Washington, having completely dropped the ball on getting the U.S. military into Afghanistan, was now engaging in the time-honored tradition of passing the buck.[74] Not surprisingly, Schroen lost his cool and exploded. He was way out on a limb and desperate for support. He did not need bureaucratic games; he needed results.

Ultimately, the first U.S. Army Special Forces A-team, ODA 555, did not arrive in Afghanistan until the evening of October 19, 2001, almost a full month behind the CIA personnel that landed with Schroen. By the time ODA 555 arrived, the CIA already had a second team on the ground, working in the area around Mazar-i-Sharif.

I am not Special Forces. I never went through the Q course at Bragg, and I have never served on an ODA. I have, however, known a lot of Special Forces operators and worked in the field with some outstanding individuals from that side of the house.

I can guarantee you that the delay in getting U.S. Army Green Berets on the ground inside Afghanistan had nothing to do with any individual's reluctance to get into the fight. In fact, I would be willing to bet that the men of ODA 555 probably had their gear packed and were ready to go to war before the sun went down on September 11, 2001.

The delay in the deployment of U.S. military forces was caused by bureaucracy and a top-heavy command structure that required every decision to be endlessly debated, staffed, briefed, and rebriefed. It was the same reason that a simple request I made for the provision of limited military support to an asset meeting and a snatch operation turned into something resembling the planning of the D-Day invasion of Normandy.

You can't run intelligence and covert action operations this way. You will end up with a lot of shiny toys and stacks of high-speed, low-drag operators, and they will accomplish very, very little. In the world of intelligence, in many cases, less is more.

I ran into exactly the same kind of issues as Schroen when I took the first American team into northern Iraq to begin preparations for the invasion of Iraq. The plan for the invasion had already been formulated: We knew that the 10th Special Forces Group out of Fort Carson was to move into northern Iraq and pave the way for the introduction of the 4th Infantry Division. We also knew that 10th Group personnel from one of their pilot teams would be accompanying us when we entered Iraq. We had met these individuals and visited Fort Carson, and some of these personnel were, in fact, already participating in preparations for deployment.

The fact remained that when we rolled into Iraq for the first time in July of 2002 all the issues concerning 10th Group participation remained unresolved. Individuals from the military side of the house with whom we had been training and working for months stayed behind. Eight CIA officers made the initial crossing, and our Special Forces brethren did not join us until October. No one could even untangle the issues concerning use of military aircraft. We drove in, riding in commercial vehicles purchased locally for this purpose.

Maybe the best-known example of the impact of this kind of inertia and delay is what happened at Tora Bora. Reading accounts of what occurred there in the fall of 2001 makes you want to cry in frustration. To this day, individuals I know who were members of that team can hardly talk about the missed opportunities without breaking down. Plain and simple, we cornered bin Laden and his senior subordinates, and then we let them walk away.

The Jawbreaker team under Gary Berntsen's team was operating on a shoestring and a prayer in pursuing al-Qaeda into Tora Bora. They had a handful of individuals on the ground, some very questionable Afghan allies, and a transport and logistical system that depended heavily on the use of ancient discarded Soviet equipment and mules. It did not matter, because Jawbreaker had something a lot more powerful and valuable than any high technology: They had a singular focus on mission accomplishment and the willingness to do whatever it took to get the job done.

At some point in that pursuit, however, it became clear that in order to prevent the escape of the fleeing senior al-Qaeda personnel, it would be necessary to introduce American ground forces to block escape routes, close with the enemy, and finish them. Specifically, in Berntsen's mind, what was needed was at least one battalion of Rangers.[75]

If you have never dealt with the Rangers, let me assure you as to their quality, their mettle, and their willingness to take on the seemingly impossible. These are men who will go anywhere, accomplish the mission no matter what the odds, and make whatever foe they are pitted against regret the day he confronted the United States of America. If anyone had told a Ranger battalion commander to take his men into Tora Bora, he would have responded simply by asking what time the aircraft was taking off. They would not have had any problem getting men to go in. They might have had a problem with men from other units trying to hitch a ride and get into the fight. These guys joined the U.S. Army to destroy our enemies; a trip to the back of beyond and a chance to kill al-Qaeda would have been a dream come true.

No one gave the order. Senior officers deliberated. Briefings were conducted. Meetings were scheduled. Staff officers worked overtime to prepare PowerPoint presentations and update SITREPs. Bin Laden and his key lieutenants walked out, and years later we are still trying to find many of these individuals, including bin Laden himself.

Three months after bin Laden's escape, the U.S. military launched an operation into the same area. Using elements of the 101st Airborne and the 10th Mountain Division, they succeeded in killing hundreds of enemy fighters. The last al-Qaeda sanctuary in Afghanistan was destroyed.[76] But not a single one of the top al-Qaeda leaders was killed or captured. It was a carefully crafted, well-executed punch, thrown three months too late.

Lest my comments be interpreted as suggesting that all the issues concerning other entities' involvement in intelligence and covert-action operations are confined to the U.S. military, let's talk about the FBI for a while and its move into the world of human intelligence operations.

There is a fair amount of friction between the CIA and the FBI. It sort of goes with the territory. Both organizations are staffed with hard-charging, proud individuals used to getting their own way. That said, cooperation between the two is considerably better today than it has been in the past, and I have worked with a great number of FBI colleagues whom I continue to view as close personal friends as well as fellow professionals.

The two organizations are fundamentally different. They are constructed from the ground up for completely different jobs. They have different cultures, and they recruit very different types of individuals. The stereotypical CIA case officer is an individual who is at home with ambiguity and change and who expects that the plan for an op may very well have to reformulated three times en route to an agent meeting. The stereotypical FBI agent is a guy in a dark suit and a white shirt who has the patience and attention to detail to spend years piecing together a complex criminal case out of a pile of minute facts and then ensure that it stands up to the intense standards of a criminal prosecution.

Having the CIA get into the business of criminal investigation would be a horrific idea. Leaving aside for the moment the significant constitutional-rights issues involved, the agency does not have the structure, focus, or personnel to carry out this task. It might ultimately reach the right conclusions, but it would be absolutely incapable of presenting those conclusions in an organized, evidentiary manner that would allow for prosecution and conviction.

It is an equally terrible idea to have the FBI begin to move into the realm of HUMINT collection. In a world that requires speed and flexibility, the FBI is a stiff, slow-moving entity completely incapable of responding as required. And yet the FBI is moving into HUMINT operations and not in a small way. It has jumped in with both feet.

Let me illustrate how ineffective this is with an example of an important terrorist case on which I was working shortly before my retirement from the CIA.

A few years ago a unit under my command developed information regarding interest on the part of a terrorist organization in the acquisition of material that would allow it to construct a weapon of mass destruction. This information was corroborated over time from multiple sources. As the picture was pieced together, it was also determined that at least some members of the organization in question had shown interest in the possibility of acquiring the necessary material from a specific location identified by us.

During operational meetings within the unit, we talked about a wide range of options to defeat this threat. It was not clear how long it might take this terrorist organization to acquire the material it was seeking, nor was it clear how quickly this group might be able to construct a weapon once it had this material in hand. Regardless, all things considered, it was clear that we were dealing with a real threat and that we needed to come up with a mechanism for taking the terrorists in question off the street.

The interest of this particular group in the acquisition of material from a specific location identified by us opened up a range of possibilities. In particular, some of the facts available suggested that it might be possible to cooperate with the FBI and to conduct a joint operation that would ultimately result in apprehension of the suspects and their successful prosecution. I, against the wise counsel of many fellow CIA officers, elected to do the corporate thing and bring the FBI into the case.

The first meeting with the FBI involved a handful of officers from their headquarters section that is charged with conducting operations against terrorist WMD programs. The second meeting, which took another two weeks to organize, involved a dozen participants from several different FBI components. There were a grand total of three CIA officers present. We were starting to feel outnumbered.

The third meeting took several more weeks to orchestrate. By this time, there were thirty-five FBI agents present. They represented a number of offices from their headquarters and three different field offices. CIA attendance remained static, with the same three officers working the op from our side. This meeting ended in a deadlock, not because of problems between the CIA and the FBI but because two of the field office representatives got into a shouting match and almost came to blows.

It had now been two months at least since we had asked the FBI to play. We were approaching the stage of the op where we had expected to be initiating operational activity on the street. In fact, we had not even yet gotten formal agreement from the FBI to participate nor could we even say with any real certainty exactly what piece of the FBI would do the op when or if it ever materialized.

Months passed. Our frustration grew. Intelligence continued to flow in showing that the threat was real and that the terrorist group's intent to acquire WMD capability remained as strong as ever. In frustration, I decided to attend the next meeting with the FBI personally in order to try to break the deadlock.

The conference room where the meeting took place was full. We had brought half a dozen CIA officers. There were close to forty FBI personnel present. During introductions, I lost track completely of who they all were or why they needed to be involved. I figured it was time to get down to brass tacks.

I told the FBI that we wanted to work with them and that we were excited about putting together an op that would result in prosecutions. I stressed, however, that the threat was growing and that we needed to move fast to head it off. I noted that we were still discussing generalities despite the fact that we would have hoped by this point to have the actual op well underway. I concluded by saying that as much as we wanted to work this target jointly, if we could not get moving soon, we might have to walk away and try to find a way to get to the target on our own.

There was a slight pause, and then one of the senior FBI agents responded by saying that if we wanted to walk away we should do so. He stated that he had no idea when they would be ready to proceed. He added that he expected that it would be many months yet and concluded his remarks by saying that actually he was not sure they were going to be able to put together an op at all and that it was possible that this target was just too difficult for them to take on. He closed by noting simply, "Maybe we can't do it."

The FBI agent who made these remarks had devoted decades of his life to the service of his country, as had many of the other FBI personnel present. They were good people who wanted to keep their fellow citizens safe and destroy the terrorist networks threatening our nation. They did not drag out the planning for this operation because they didn't care or because they were trying to make my life miserable. They did so because, working within the confines of the bureaucracy in which they served, they had no choice.

I was asking them for a quick decision and a commitment to an open-ended operation that would have to be put together as it progressed. In order to help they needed to spin up undercover operatives, commercial backstopping, and a host of technical and human capabilities, and they needed to do it now. They were incapable of doing that. I wanted someone to make a decision; there was no such someone. In their system they would be required to write a lengthy and complex operational proposal that ultimately might run to many hundreds of pages. This proposal would be scrutinized, edited, briefed, briefed again, and maybe, someday, far down the road, approved.

By that time, it would not matter what the result would be. Events would have passed us by. In all likelihood, the terrorist group in question would have succeeded in acquiring the capability it desired. If it had not, it would only be by the grace of God, not because of anything we had done.

I don't know what the resolution of this impasse was. As of the time I retired, almost a year after we began talking to the FBI, we still had not even reached the point of having an agreed-upon operational plan. I hope and pray that the CIA is not still waiting for the FBI to move. I hope somebody somewhere has moved.

Despite all the issues outlined above, the FBI is expanding daily the scope of its human intelligence operations. Once upon a time, there was a clear demarcation between the CIA and the FBI. In particular it used to be accepted as a cardinal principle that the FBI did not operate outside the United States. Those days are long gone. Not only does the FBI have an extensive collection of legal attachés around the world, they have moved heavily into running agents abroad as well. These operations may or may not be known to the CIA, and there may or may not be any coordination arranged.

To illustrate the kind of issues that arise when multiple human intelligence services are operating abroad, allow me to use a fairly benign example. Several years ago I was running operations in a country in Asia. Much of what we did was focused on the terrorist threat, and we had several productive operations that were ongoing with the local service against Internet cafés used by terrorists for communication purposes.

One day, while I was sitting in my office, a friend who worked for a local military command stopped by. He told me that he had some information for me that he thought I might find of interest. I asked him to have a seat, and then he told me a story about a conversation he had had the night before with a Special Forces sergeant he met in a bar downtown. In brief the sergeant told him that he was in country to do some training with the local military but that while he was in country he had also been tasked by his own chain of command to collect information on Internet cafés that might be used by terrorists for communications.

I did not hit the roof, but I was not happy. I asked my friend if he could get in touch with this sergeant. When he advised that he could, I asked him to contact the sergeant and have him come and talk to me. My friend agreed.

The next day the sergeant came to see me. He was a good man and, not surprisingly, a little chagrined that he had been called on the carpet. He explained that he had received tasking from his military command to gather information on Internet cafés in country and that it had never occurred to him that this might cause a problem of any kind.

I told the sergeant, without going into any real detail, that there were a number of joint operations with the local liaison service that were ongoing against the cafés in question. I explained to him that these businesses were in areas where no foreigners ever went. One white face would set off alarm bells and might destroy months of work. I stressed that, in fact, in operations of this type, even the slightest misstep could mean disaster.

The sergeant understood. He promised me he would stand down, and he kept his word. As I said, he was a good man.

The fact remained that but for a lucky break and an alert friend I would never have known anything until our ops started going dead and months of backbreaking work was destroyed.

There is a lot more that could be said on this topic but very little of it in an unclassified setting. Let it suffice to say at this point that we are not just talking about involving a lot of organizations in human intelligence operations who are not very good at that kind of thing. We are talking about inviting a lot of people to play in a very tight operational space with only an extremely fuzzy understanding of who is directing traffic and who is in charge. The results are predictable: Organizations will run into each other, and the results may be catastrophic.

Back in the early 1990s, Charlie Sheen made a movie called *Beyond the Law* about a police officer in the Southwest who goes undercover to infiltrate a motorcycle gang. It's not the greatest film ever made, but it is a long way from being the worst. It is, in fact, based on the true story of an officer who actually carried out such an assignment, and it does a fairly good job of illustrating the incredible challenges such work entails.

One of the scenes in that film that is burned into my memory concerns a rally in the desert. Sheen, who by this point has been accepted into the group, is present when an FBI undercover officer, also present at the rally, is detected and confronted by members of the gang. Until this moment, Sheen is unaware that there is another undercover officer at the rally. No coordination with his office has been done by the FBI. There are two separate ops being run, and they have now crossed wires. One of them has gone south in a big way, and Sheen, still desperately exposed himself, is now faced with the prospect not only of protecting his own thin cover but of trying to think of a way to save the life of the FBI undercover as well. It's a powerful scene, and if you have ever been out on the street with a gun on your ankle and no backup, you know exactly how terrifying such a moment could be.

I'll let you watch the movie if you want to find out how this all sorts out. The point for our purposes is that this is no way to run a railroad or an operation. You can't have multiple agencies fishing in the same pond and not think you are going to have problems. Things will get screwed up. Lines will cross, and people will die.

I have a good friend in the agency who worked undercover for years inside motorcycle gangs on the East Coast. He is replete with stories about similar incidents that occurred during operations in which he was involved. One of the points he makes all the time is that your tradecraft is only as good as that of the weakest element involved in operations against a target. When he went undercover, for example, he spent the better part of a year away from his department—learning to ride, being seen, even getting the right tan lines to show he had been wearing his biker attire, not a police uniform, while riding. The bike he rode was one he built himself, and he knew it inside out.

Other organizations working the same target did not take the same care. They cut corners. They used motorcycles impounded from arrested gang members, which were often recognized by bikers at rallies the undercover officers attended. They took shortcuts in prep time and often took officers only a few months away from uniformed duty and inserted them into venues where it was highly likely they would be recognized by persons they had arrested only a short time before.

The result was not simply that the operation in question was blown or that the life of an undercover officer was endangered. The result was, as we would say in the trade, that the entire area was "heated up": It was essentially advertised to the target group that they were a focus of police interest and that undercover operatives were being utilized to penetrate them. Every other undercover attempting to work the same target would pay the price in increased scrutiny and by being put through longer and more rigorous vetting procedures.

These same principles apply to undercover work of all kinds. We cannot have a random collection of junior varsity teams trying in some haphazard fashion to crawl into the depths of al-Qaeda. We need a single, highly disciplined varsity team with laserlike focus and absolute precision.

It is strange to think that we have come to this point some sixty-plus years after the founding of the OSS, because all these issues were fully understood and appreciated then. It was, in fact, precisely because of these kinds of concerns that President Franklin Roosevelt, on the advice of Donovan and over the concerted opposition of the military services, created the Coordinator of Information, which then evolved into the OSS.

Consider, for example, the memorandum from the Secretary of War implementing Roosevelt's direction that the Coordinator of Information should be established on September 6, 1941:

> ***Subject: Undercover Intelligence Service***
>
> *The military and naval intelligence services have gone into the field of undercover intelligence to a limited extent. In the view of the appointment of the Coordinator of Information and the work which it is understood the President desires him to undertake, it is believed that the undercover intelligence of the two services should be consolidated under the Coordinator of Information. The reasons for this are that an undercover intelligence organization is much more effective if under one head than three, and that a civilian agency, such as the Coordinator of Information, has distinct advantages over any military or naval agency in the administration of such a service.*[77]

Roosevelt was not simply creating a new intelligence service; he was creating a service that would control all undercover strategic-level HUMINT intelligence operations, and he knew exactly why he was doing it.

Kermit Roosevelt, in writing the official war history of the OSS, had this to say on the issue of whether a civilian or a military organization should run HUMINT operations:

> *Secret intelligence, sabotage and subversion could not be run along standard military or bureaucratic lines. In the handling of agents the human element was primary, and it was discovered many times over that a few individuals who combined understanding of this factor with imagination in operations and objectivity in evaluating results could produce far better intelligence than could larger staffs which attempted to work on a more regular, more bureaucratic or more military basis.*
>
> *Although external factors accounted for much, the notably disparate results of various competing OSS units attested the validity of the principle. Such a contrast was provided by the large but relatively unproductive SI/London staff compared with the small SI/Algiers unit which provided for Operation ANVIL, the best briefed invasion in history, as much information as the British and French services combined.*[78]

Sixty-seven years after Roosevelt and Donovan reached their conclusions about how to run effective human intelligence operations, we seem determined to relearn all the old lessons the hard way. In the midst of an open-ended worldwide conflict against a fanatical foe, as the advance of technology threatens to arm our enemies with weapons of unspeakable power, we may not have the luxury of taking our time in getting this right. The fact that we have allowed our existing strategic human intelligence organization, the CIA, to deteriorate does not mean that we were not right about the necessity to have one such single, flexible, civilian entity. We do not need a return to the chaos and confusion that characterized intelligence collection in the 1930s. We need a new OSS.

CHAPTER EIGHT

If One Cook Is Good, Ten Must Be Better

In 1944 Ray Peers, the commanding officer of OSS Detachment 101 in Burma, was faced with a difficult decision. Detachment 101's operations had mushroomed since it was established about a year before. The pace of work had increased dramatically. Peers, operating from the headquarters of the detachment in the rear, was having an increasingly difficult time keeping up with all the ops that were ongoing. He had men spread over thousands of miles of jungle; he had four separate sectors under his command, and within each sector he had any number of small bases and independent teams, many of them in only intermittent communication with his headquarters element. Peers's staff was limited, and it was about all he could do just to keep a stream of fresh men and supplies headed downrange.

So Peers did something very bold and infinitely practical. He delegated significant amounts of his authority to each of the four sector commanders and empowered them to make decisions about operations in their respective areas. He explained to them that he judged that they were better informed than he was of the situation on the ground and that he trusted their judgment. Operations, already moving quickly, picked up even further, and there were successes against the Japanese in all areas.[79]

Now maybe that all sounds like common sense. And actually, it is. It is worth noting, however, what Peers did not do.

He did not write a cable to Washington and request an increase in the size of his staff so that he could more properly and fully review all proposed operations. He did not inform his sector commanders that they would henceforth have to complete longer and more detailed volumes of paperwork so that he could gain a better picture of the details of each of their proposals. He did not suggest that the operational pace would have to be slowed so that headquarters could keep up.

Peers trusted his people. He had good men in charge, and he held them to a high standard. He provided the strategic guidance they needed to do their jobs, shoveled them the support they required, and then he got out of their way. The results were astounding. In terms of both intelligence production and covert action, the record of Detachment 101 was on a par with anything the OSS accomplished anywhere else in the world. When Merrill's Marauders made their famous march across Burma to attack Myitkyina they did so based on intelligence provided by Peers's men and with the continuous operational and logistical support of Detachment 101 and the Kachin Rangers working with them. That movement would have been impossible without that cooperation.

Within the CIA the basic principles that guided Peers seem to have been forgotten. We do not react to problems by relieving leaders who fail to perform and replacing them with individuals who can. We react by creating new bureaucracies, drawing lines on charts, and requiring ever-greater degrees of "coordination" and "review."

Consider, for example, the case of the Counterterrorist Center (CTC) within the CIA. This is the entity that, with very few exceptions, is charged with the pursuit of all terrorist organizations worldwide. It is a huge edifice composed of thousands of individuals and with a budget of tens of millions of dollars. When the president asks how the hunt for Osama bin Laden is going, he is asking for a report on the performance of this outfit.

CTC owns no turf; it controls no stations. Its primary area of operations at present is in the Middle East and South Asia.

All this real estate is controlled, for CIA purposes, by another bureaucratic entity, the Near East and South Asia Division (NE). NE owns all the stations and bases in this part of the world. All the chiefs of station in this region are put in place by the chief of the NE Division, evaluated by him, and answerable to him. None of them is under the command of CTC.

So when CTC wants to run an op in Afghanistan, it is required to coordinate with the NE Division. The proposal for such an operation will, in fact, have to be staffed through not only all the applicable CTC desks at headquarters but will also have to be staffed through all the NE desks as well. When the proposal reaches a station in the field, it will be read by a chief of station who does not work for CTC but does answer directly to the NE Division. The career prospects of this COS will be directly tied to how he is evaluated by his superiors within the NE Division. CTC has no input whatsoever on that score. If NE and CTC see eye to eye, there will not be an issue. But if CTC wants to make a bold, aggressive move and the NE Division prefers a more cautious approach that is less likely to risk relations with the host government, it is not hard to predict how the COS will come down on the question.

Even if there is no significant difference of opinion on how to proceed, simply the task of getting messages moved is now so complex and burdensome that it produces a major drag on operations. It is not uncommon to find that a cable to the field from a headquarters desk will have to be seen and chopped on by dozens of separate desks before it can be transmitted. Every one of those desks may request changes, impose objections, or, horror of all horrors, ask for a meeting to discuss how to proceed. Meanwhile, somewhere in the field, a real terrorist is building a real bomb, and people are getting ready to die.

How did we get to this situation?

Back in the 1980s it became apparent that the CIA was not doing enough against terrorism. Palestinian terrorist groups and Hizbullah were beginning to be seen as real threats. The CIA had traditionally focused on the threat from the Soviet Union, and terrorist groups were not seen as a primary target for collection. This needed to change.

One reasonable course of action would have been to charge the existing geographic-area divisions with pursuit of this target, give them the resources to tackle the job, and hold them accountable for producing results but otherwise get out of their way. This is certainly the way Ray Peers would have handled it. It would have left a single individual in each part of the world—for example, the chief of the NE Division in the Middle East—accountable for success or failure.

Unfortunately, this was not done. An entirely new apparatus, layered on top of the old, was constructed, and issues and conflicts between the two structures were now to be resolved through coordination, discussion, meetings, and cooperation. When or if the two competing bureaucracies could not resolve differences they might have, issues would be bumped up to the next level of command for resolution.

For reasons that remain mysterious to me, despite the obvious problems with this cumbersome arrangement, this type of structure was then replicated over the years for other issues. There now exist within the CIA a Counterproliferation Center, a Counternarcotics Center, and a Counterintelligence Center. Therefore, at present, if you are the chief of the NE Division, you are not actually accountable for any of the operations in your area against terrorist groups, nuclear smuggling networks, state WMD programs, or drug-smuggling cartels. One might be excused, I think, for wondering, given the current intelligence priorities, what targets the NE Division is charged to pursue.

The excessively cumbersome and inefficient bureaucratic arrangements within the CIA are only the tip of the iceberg. Post-9/11, the changes that have been made in the bureaucratic structure of the intelligence community, writ large, dwarf anything within the CIA in both scale and impact. The Bush administration, led by Republicans who claim to be the champions of small government and private enterprise, created vast new legions of bureaucrats whose job it was to ride desks, generate process, and add little or nothing to the actual business of intelligence collection.

We have just finished discussing the role of the CIA's Counterterrorism Center and how that organization was created atop an already existing structure of area divisions within CIA. Since 9/11, however, we have created, in addition to the CIA's CTC, a National Counterterrorism Center (NCTC) as well. NCTC runs no operations. It sits atop the CTC charged with strategic-level terrorist analysis and strategic planning of all counterterrorism activities. Both of these activities were, until the creation of the NCTC, already being done by CTC. Once NCTC has finished thinking deep thoughts about what we should do in the way of counterterrorism operations, it coordinates these concepts with CTC, which, of course, then attempts to coordinate them with the NE Division, which actually owns the personnel who will run the operations in question. A lot of paper is consumed, and a lot of meetings are held. In the meantime, the same relative handful of ops officers downrange in the nasty places of the world are actually doing the work of meeting assets and preventing attacks.

NCTC is, of course, filled with a lot of good, well-intentioned people, and to the extent it has facilitated communication among agencies, that is a positive. The point, however, is that we did not need the creation of a new bureaucracy to make people cooperate and share information. All we needed to do was give the order and hold people accountable for complying with it. The first time we fired a senior-level manager in the CIA or the FBI for failing to cooperate, coordinate, and share intelligence, we would have gotten the message across. I suspect attitudes would have changed markedly in a very short period of time.

If what I have described above sounds like a very complicated, inefficient mess, then I have done a good job of describing it. On a good day the net impact of all this additional bureaucracy is nil. On a bad day in the field ops are at a standstill because all available officers are answering cables from headquarters requesting input for an assessment being written by a bureaucratic entity no one has ever heard of and whose utility remains unknown. During World War II General Stilwell used to say that his solution to Pentagon interference in his ops in the field was to walk through the halls of the building, hand every other man a rifle, and order him to the front. A similar solution might be of great utility within the bowels of this vast, wasteful "counterterrorist" bureaucracy.

But wait, there's more.

Prior to 9/11 the director of the Central Intelligence Agency was also nominally the head of the Intelligence Community. In practice he had almost no authority to implement this mandate. He could not actually order the heads of the other intelligence agencies to do much of anything, and most importantly from a federal government perspective, he did not control their budgets.

Post-9/11, everyone agreed, for a whole host of perfectly good reasons, that this could not go on. Therefore, the position of director of National Intelligence (DNI) was created. This individual was given exactly the same responsibility that the director of the CIA had always had. He was named as the head of the Intelligence Community. He was not, however, given significantly more power. A few minor changes were made, but on balance the DNI was left in largely the same situation as the director of the CIA had always been—without the power to do his job. In particular, with regard to the biggest pieces of the intelligence budget, which are contained within the Department of Defense, the DNI was given no budgetary authority.

What the DNI was given was a staff. At last count this staff numbered somewhere in the neighborhood of four thousand individuals. That is four thousand new bureaucrats in an office that until this recent "reform" did not exist. Not a single one of them runs operations. Not a single one of them recruits assets or produces intelligence. What they do produce, however, is process, lots of it.

A few years prior to my retirement, and post-9/11, I was serving as the chief of station in a country abroad. I was regularly visited by delegations of well-meaning individuals from the DNI's office or NCTC who came TDY to station to discuss with me and my officers "important" initiatives they had underway. At the risk of sounding snide, let me describe to you how these visits would typically go.

I would receive a message in cable traffic advising that several individuals from some office of which I had never heard were coming to station to meet with me. If I had the time in my very busy schedule, I would send a note or make a call to try to find out who these individuals were and why they were coming. Like as not, the desk officer to whom I spoke would have no idea and would be unable to provide any clarification.

A few weeks later the delegation in question would arrive in station, and I would meet with them in my office. They would likely all be well intentioned, well educated, and eager to serve their nation. But none of them would be professional intelligence officers. They might be former Department of Agriculture types or retired military or any manner of things, but none of them would have any idea how intelligence operations were run, how terrorists operated, or even how a station functioned.

These individuals would begin by asking me if I had read the "book cable" they had sent outlining the purpose of their project. I would admit that I had not, because I had not received it. They would look puzzled and indicate that it should have come through weeks before. In most cases, it would turn out later that their message had never been transmitted out of headquarters, because they did not actually understand how the communications system worked and had never gotten anyone to release it.

Once we were past this awkward moment, the team would then brief me on their project, which invariably would be one of those concepts that sounds great to people in Washington who have never been overseas but is immediately apparent as having no utility of any kind to operators who have spent time downrange. It might, for example, be a proposal to work with the local liaison service to collect intelligence on a particular radical religious sect but ignored the fact that the head of the service was a member of the sect, intimately involved in its activities, and, therefore, highly unlikely to agree to work with us against it. It might be a proposal to fund a program with the local government to collect data on commercial ship traffic between the nation in question and Iran, but ignored the fact that there was no such ship traffic and that Iranians were generally not permitted to enter the country. It might be a proposal to help the locals acquire some sort of technical intercept capability that sounded great but would first require the local telecommunications infrastructure to be significantly upgraded, a task unlikely to be completed for another ten years.

In the end the team would leave and move on to their next stop. Before they left country I would try to spring time to take them shopping in the local *souq* (the marketplace) or beg my long-suffering wife to do so. We would do our best to make sure the team understood that we respected their desire to be of service to their country. We would try hard to conceal our confusion as to how initiatives of this type were going to help us win the war on terror. Then we would drive them to the airport, get back to work, and think about all the things we might be able to accomplish if those four thousand bodies had been case officers sent downrange to run operations instead of bureaucrats parked behind desks and told to generate paper.

When I returned home to headquarters after my last PCS field assignment, I found that the situation was not any better there. I was placed in charge of the unit within the CIA that was charged with pursuit of all terrorist WMD programs worldwide. Any nonstate actor on the planet who was playing with nuclear, radiological, chemical, or biological weapons was our problem. It was, needless to say, a daunting assignment.

Within my team there was an operational wing and an analytical wing. The operational wing, composed of those individuals actually involved in supporting field ops against terrorist targets, was chronically understaffed. Those people that we did have were generally short on experience and training. Despite this, the stations and bases we were supporting were so strapped for resources themselves that I was often forced to surge officers out of my headquarters-based team to run operations in the field. In effect, we were forced to jump on a plane and go do the ops ourselves, because there simply was no one available downrange to do it.

The analytical wing included a large body of colocated NCTC analysts and, as a consequence, was substantially larger than the ops wing. Its personnel overall were also more experienced and better trained. On many occasions this disparity was such that I ended up employing a certain amount of bureaucratic sleight of hand, "stealing" analysts from NCTC for the purpose of sending them overseas to assist with operations. In other cases, when I was unable to pull this off, analysts literally sat without sufficient work because there were too many of them to handle the relatively small quantity of intelligence coming in from ops overseas.

None of this is intended to be a criticism of any of the individual officers involved, who were, by and large, smart, capable, patriotic individuals. I am simply trying to point out the futility of responding to a failure in the collection of intelligence by enlarging headquarters components; creating new agencies, staffs, and centers; and neglecting the field in the process. There may be thousands of new bureaucrats in Washington all calling themselves "intelligence officers," but in some nasty Third World post ten thousand miles away, where new Islamic extremists are being spawned every day, there are still a handful of real ops officers who are increasingly pressed for time to run real ops by the necessity to feed the bureaucratic beast back home.

Committees and staffs are, I am sure, good for many things. They are of no value in the conduct of human intelligence operations. What is needed for effective HUMINT ops are speed, flexibility, and creativity. A handful of the right men and women with the appropriate authorities can come up with a plan to steal the crown jewels in a matter of days. One hundred "experts" in a rigid bureaucratic structure will still be "staffing" the problem a year later.

Late in the summer of 2002, I was sitting inside Iraq near the border between the area controlled by the Patriotic Union of Kurdistan (PUK), a friendly Kurdish group, and the territory under the control of Ansar al-Islam, an al-Qaeda affiliate. With me were seven other CIA officers, and our mission was to collect on the activities of Ansar in general, the influx of al-Qaeda fighters fleeing Afghanistan, and possible chemical- and biological-weapons programs centered around a village called Sargat.

All the gear we needed for that deployment we carried in two Land Rover–type vehicles. We lived out of a concrete-block building in which the cook made dinner on the kitchen floor, the plumbing worked sporadically, and it was absolutely raging hot at all times. We did all our work around one table in one room, ate whatever was available in local markets, and slept with our weapons by our sides to ensure security in the event it turned out our local hosts had been penetrated and the guards outside the door turned against us.

During a deployment of roughly two and a half months, we generated somewhere in excess of one thousand intelligence reports. We interrogated dozens of captured Ansar and al-Qaeda personnel, sent large numbers of sources inside Ansar territory, mapped every position of significance there down to ten-digit grid coordinates, and acquired chapter and verse on al-Qaeda's presence, Ansar capabilities, and the status of ongoing terrorist WMD programs. Had the Bush administration given the go-ahead to implement our attack plan, we also would have killed or captured all the Ansar and al-Qaeda personnel then hiding in that area.

The point of this story is not to highlight the achievements of this particular team; it is to illustrate how intelligence operations are run. The team in question did superb work, but many teams before it had done similar things, and many others have done so since. This is how human intelligence operations are done: by small groups of highly trained, select individuals who are entrusted with the necessary authorities and capabilities to get their jobs done.

We could have augmented our team with all sorts of additional personnel and bells and whistles. We could have added equipment and weapons. We could have dedicated a team of analysts and targeting officers back in Washington to review our traffic and provide guidance and direction. We could, in short, have transformed this very small, very agile team into a large, ponderous "task force" of some kind that would, on paper, have appeared significantly more impressive. In so doing, we would have killed any chance of actually accomplishing our mission.

There is an old adage, which has nothing to do with espionage: "Too many cooks spoil the broth." It is based on a very simple, common sense notion. Cooking is art. To do it right requires a rare combination of skills and abilities in one gifted individual. You cannot do it by committee.

Espionage, too, is an art, not a science. Find the best artists, give them sufficient guidance so they know what it is you need them to create, then get out of their way and stop reaching over their shoulders. The results will astound you.

CHAPTER NINE

A New OSS

We are, as I write, in the midst of at least two wars. The North Koreans are pushing ahead with their mad race toward oblivion. Iran is torn with turmoil and still claiming the right to arm itself with nuclear arms. Pakistan hovers on the edge of anarchy. Russia may be moving toward democracy or sliding backward into some form of militant fascism. The Chinese are methodically infiltrating our most sensitive computer systems.

We cannot afford to continue to accept a human intelligence apparatus which regularly fails when confronted with its most important missions. We cannot continue to hope that playing with lines on a wiring diagram or adding more staff officers in Washington will fix our problems. We need to act decisively now, before the next disaster, before the next horrific attack on our soil.

These are my ideas on how to do that. They are not half measures or arguments for gradual change. They are, I hope, collectively, a blueprint for a new OSS, an organization capable of grappling with and defeating the dragons we confront today.

1. START OVER:

Personnel issues alone make it impossible to repair the existing structure of the Central Intelligence Agency. The sails have been patched and the holes in the hull plugged as many times as is possible. We need a new vessel.

The operational ranks of the CIA contain significant numbers of officers who have been converted from other specialties to fill gaps created by budget and personnel cuts. The rationale behind this kind of stopgap measure is understandable. That said, however, it has resulted in a dilution of the talent pool. The guy sitting next to me may be a world-class athlete and a Rhodes scholar; he may also be a former logistics officer who went through an abbreviated ops familiarization course and has never actually recruited an asset in his life. He may well have forgotten more than I will ever know about how to keep a forward operating base supplied. It is highly unlikely that he will prove to be an effective operations officer. We cannot win a war with this kind of uneven quality.

We have also allowed overall medical and physical standards to evaporate. If I am on a team in a remote area, I may be working with individuals who can survive in the wild for extended periods of time and are capable of successfully escaping and evading under extreme conditions. I may also have on my team an individual who is grossly overweight and a diabetic who will die horribly the moment we are cut off from regular resupply and who has no hope whatsoever of moving overland on his own power for even a short distance.

The impact of personnel shortfalls and the war on terror has also meant that new officers have been promoted with exceptional speed. The GS-14 on my team in a war zone abroad may have fifteen years of service throughout the Middle East to her credit. She may also, if she has been lucky, have no more than five years' service and be on her first PCS overseas tour. The gulf between the two levels of experience is mammoth, and while energy and talent can fill a lot of gaps, there are also many lessons that can only be learned with experience.

Language capacity, always an issue, has been allowed to atrophy. Officers are no longer steeped in the folklore, culture, and traditions of the nations in which they work. They shuttle from assignment to assignment, punching tickets and focused on career advancement. Increasingly, our intelligence officers are incapable of pushing beyond a small circle of English-speaking contacts and communicating with the key target groups against which they must operate.

The biggest issue here, though, is bureaucratic and has to do with the nature of federal government personnel systems and individual rights. We can change CIA medical standards tomorrow, but we cannot retroactively begin to require as conditions of employment standards that were never previously required or made an element of a particular job or profession. Realistically, neither can we wade into an agency and summarily demote large numbers of individuals or move them out of career tracks in which they have served, in their eyes successfully, for many years. The result would be widespread litigation and uproar.

Even if we were to design some mechanism for attempting to slice and dice the existing structure and for moving individuals around, the obvious impact on morale would be catastrophic. If I am a GS-15 former polygrapher who is now serving in a senior management position as an operations officer, I am highly unlikely to accept any rationale that necessitates my accepting a two-grade demotion and a return to my previous line of work. I am going to quit, or I am going to file a lawsuit, or I am simply going to stack arms and retire on the job, but I am not going to accept such a change happily and eagerly.

Just as importantly, though, even if somehow we could suspend the laws of personal behavior and make this happen, we would not want the resulting creation. We might have a reshaped and retooled CIA. We would not have a new OSS.

There are many magnificent people in the CIA of today. Given the obstacles they have to overcome, some of the things they do, each and every day, are almost beyond belief. Overall, though, as has been discussed herein at length, what we have today is an organization that has lost much of what made the OSS such a dynamic and creative entity. On some level this is more than just a decline in standards or changes in personnel structure. It is spiritual.

The OSS made a religion out of placing mission accomplishment, speed, and effectiveness above all else. It did not care one whit about the school solution or what the "book" said. In 1944 an OSS air unit was stationed in England in support of the operations of OSS teams on the ground inside occupied France. One day a line lieutenant from a nearby army unit arrived at the OSS compound, asked to see the colonel in charge, and then lodged a formal complaint to the effect that OSS personnel refused to salute him when they passed him on the nearby airbase. The OSS commander responded without hesitation, saying, "Why the hell should they salute you? They don't even salute me." He then instructed the lieutenant to get out and not to come back.[80]

The Colonel had no interest whatsoever in form, process, or military courtesy. He wanted individuals who thought for themselves and would get the job done no matter what the cost. Those who have spent a career in today's CIA, plodding forward through an increasingly rigid bureaucratic structure, all too often fail to measure up.

The OSS drew individuals from all walks of life, and it relied heavily upon the breadth of this experience to find ways forward, even against the steepest of odds. Out of this mixture of backgrounds, skills, and outlooks might come some very bizarre proposals. Just as easily, however, what was created might be pure magic. We are not going to duplicate that kind of genius by simply repackaging a federal bureaucracy. We will need many individuals out of the CIA in a new OSS, but we will equally value those persons who come from the military, academia, and private industry and who know nothing about how the CIA used to operate.

2. KEEP IT SMALL:

Elite organizations are so called because they are small, have high standards, and are staffed by a select number of individuals with a rare combination of skills. You cannot mass-produce this. If you increase the size of the NBA to 150 teams and let them carry fifty men on a roster, you will end up with a semipro basketball league. The original OSS was about thirteen thousand strong. That is probably as good a number as any to use for a benchmark in building the new organization.

Washington bureaucrats have a tendency to believe that any problem can be solved simply by throwing more money and more people at it. This is easy. We have lots of money, and we have lots of people. In fact, though, especially in intelligence work, more people and more money may not only *not* solve the problem, they may exacerbate it. With a larger organization comes not only a dilution of talent but also more bureaucracy. Agility and speed are everything in intel work and all the more so when we are talking about counterterrorist operations. We do not need or want a chain saw to do the work of a scalpel.

If I am in Afghanistan tomorrow with a handful of men, and I acquire information that a tribal chief wishes to provide information on the location of Osama bin Ladin, what I need, first and foremost, is to get in front of that individual as quickly as possible. Of course, I need to be smart about how I do it. I need to ensure I do not walk into an ambush, and I need to take care of my people. I also need to approach this new potential source professionally. The fact that he tells me something does not make it so. Maybe he is a liar. Maybe he is working against me. Maybe he believes everything he is saying but has himself been duped. I will need to work all of this out, test his information, and, as is always true in espionage, watch my back at all times.

What I do not need is interference and delay imposed from above. If Washington believes I am incapable of accurately assessing the situation and acting with due prudence, they should relieve me. What they should not do is ask me to sit tight while ten thousand miles away several hundred people who have never been to Afghanistan, are lucky if they could find it on a map, and would not know an op from a hole in the ground second-guess every move I make.

What I do not need is endless communication asking me for more and more detail on how I propose to proceed. I will make a plan. I will take all the threats seriously. That said, however, the reality is that, of necessity, my plan will begin to change as soon as I leave the office, and it will morph even more radically as soon as I make contact with the source and begin to acquire more details.

In short, this kind of work cannot be done according to standard procedures or subject to control by large staffs and legions of reviewers, coordinators, and second-guessers. It can only be done by small bodies of highly trained individuals entrusted with freedom of action. Either I move now or there is likely no point in moving at all.

3. KEEP IT FLAT:

Bureaucrats believe that even the most intractable of problems can be solved by the addition of a few lines to a wiring diagram, an increase in staff, and a demand for enhanced coordination. These days the halls of CIA headquarters are filled with well-meaning individuals extolling the virtues of "cross-walking" proposals around the "community," "synergy," and "deep dives" into complex issues by "multidisciplinary" blue-ribbon panels and "brain trusts." Managers go for days doing nothing but running from one meeting to the next and reviewing "spot reports" and memoranda.

None of these things has any connection to the running of operations. None of them is getting us any closer to catching Osama bin Laden or stopping the proliferation of nuclear material. None of them is going to help us predict the next Russian attack on Georgia. We will not penetrate the Iranian nuclear weapons program by thinking really hard about it.

I know a fellow in the agency who used to say that our best bet for defeating al-Qaeda was to convince them to adopt our own bureaucratic procedures. He figured if Osama used our planning process, he would still be trying to work the proposal for the 9/11 attacks through al-Qaeda committees. The fellow was being sarcastic, of course. He was also horribly, horribly right.

What we need is the simplest, flattest structure possible, with authority and capability delegated to the lowest possible level. The post-9/11 push to require ever-greater degrees of coordination and discussion prior to the initiation of any significant action must be reversed. This is taking us in exactly the wrong direction. We do not need more discussion. We need more movement.

Part of the answer is ensuring that a new OSS has the broadest, clearest possible mandate and then letting it run. Part of the answer, though, is ensuring that its internal structure remains clean and straightforward. We cannot allow the kind of bureaucratic structure that has come to characterize today's CIA to creep into the OSS. Ray Peers's approach was dead on: Put good men and women in place, hand them the authority and resources they need to do the job, and then get out of their way. If they fail to produce, relieve them; otherwise let them be.

It is impossible to fully diagram the organization of a new OSS in advance of the making of key decisions by national command authority about its size, scope, and mission. As a straw man, however, I would suggest the following:

A. Operational Department A – North Africa, the Middle East, the Horn of Africa, and South Asia as far east as Bangladesh, including Afghanistan, Pakistan, and India. This would correspond roughly to the area covered by the military's CENTCOM. Within this area Department A would have responsibility for all operations against all targets. It would cover, among other things, questions of internal stability, nuclear proliferation, terrorism, and narcotics trafficking to the extent that it is considered a task within the purview of the OSS. There would be no separate centers, such as the current CIA Counterterrorist Center. The man or woman running Department A would have the power and authority to go after all targets in his or her area of operations. This person would also be held responsible for the success or failure of all operations. These same principles would apply to all operational departments within the OSS.

B. Operational Department B – Russia, Ukraine, Belarus, Moldavia, the Caucasus, and the former Soviet Republics in Central Asia

C. Operational Department C – China and North Korea

D. Operational Department D – All of East Asia other than China and North Korea

E. Operational Department E – All of Africa not included within Department A

F. Operational Department F – Latin America

G. Operational Department G – Europe, to include Eastern Europe and the Baltic States

4. SELECT FOR LEADERSHIP AND PUT IN PLACE AN EXPERT TRACK FOR THOSE INDIVIDUALS WHO WANT TO REMAIN FOCUSED ON PERFORMANCE OF INDIVIDUAL SKILLS:

Discard the current system, in which individuals are rewarded for excellence in individual achievement by being made into managers and leaders. Put in place a system that selects those individuals who want to manage and have demonstrated ability to do so and then trains them in how to discharge this responsibility properly. This should not be a one-week charm school or seminar. It ought to be a course of several months' duration that not only teaches and educates but also tests how badly the individual seeking to be a manager wants to take on that responsibility.

Those individuals who do not wish to manage and lead but would prefer to continue with a career dedicated to excellence in the performance of individual skills should be given the opportunity to do so. There should, for instance, be a track through Senior Intelligence Service (SIS)–equivalent grades for case officers, so that they can continue to be promoted and rewarded as experts without being forced to take on leadership and management roles for which they may be ill suited.

If we follow such a path, we might find in a few years that a typical field station is run by someone who knows how to lead and manage and enjoys doing so and that this chief of station has at his disposal not simply a collection of junior case officers but also seasoned, experienced veterans who are free to focus on individual cases and operations, not administration and embassy relations. Not only would these be individuals with extensive operational experience, they would likely also be officers with many years of service on the ground in the nation where they were assigned. They would speak the language fluently, and they would understand the customs, traditions, and culture. They would serve as a huge reservoir of institutional knowledge. Such a result would be a vast improvement over the current situation.

5. INSTITUTIONALIZE THE TRAINING OF LEADERS AND MANAGERS AND ENFORCE STANDARDS OF PERFORMANCE AND BEHAVIOR:

As noted above, we need to move to a system in which leaders are selected based on criteria other than the performance of individual skills. We then need to train them in how to discharge their duties. Beyond this, though, we need to put in place an entire career progression for leaders and managers that rewards them based on how well they perform in this capacity and that also continues to train and guide them as they progress through the ranks. The U.S. military has such a system in place; it takes officers at various pivotal junctures in their careers and puts them through successive courses of instruction keyed to the challenges they will face at each level in normal career progression. This is a good model for the CIA or a successor organization to use in putting together its own such training program.

Officers selected and trained as managers and leaders would be pulled out of their line assignments at designated points in their careers and put through successive courses designed to prepare them for the next move up the ladder. For example, certainly, in preparation for the jump to the equivalent of what is today Senior Intelligence Service rank, officers would be put into a resident course of two to three months' duration. This course would not simply teach them organizational structure and principles; it would reinforce the continuing message of their responsibility as leaders to their subordinates. It would contain healthy doses of instruction on ethics, decision making, accepting responsibility, and so on.

Such a course would also not be simply a box-checking exercise. A passing grade would not be automatic. In fact, probably nothing could be better for the overall health of a new OSS than for a few select individuals periodically to be washed out of a course such as this for failing to demonstrate that necessary work ethic or dedication to their responsibilities. As noted elsewhere in many places in this narrative, standards do not mean much if you don't enforce them.

Having established a core of leaders and managers who were selected as such and trained as such, the organization should then ensure that they maintain the standards expected of them. Punish officers who do not fulfill their obligations and who abuse their positions. In the course of my career in the Central Intelligence Agency, on innumerable occasions I heard speeches delivered by senior officials regarding "zero tolerance" for all sorts of transgressions. Shortly prior to my retirement, I remember vividly reading what was probably the tenth message I had seen saying that senior managers who were found to have engaged in sexual liaisons with junior officers under their command would be shown no leniency and could expect to be dismissed from the service.

I am unaware of even a single incident in which such a standard was actually upheld. On the contrary, I, and any other agency officer who has not been asleep for the last twenty years, could readily name at least a dozen senior officers infamous for having sexual relationships with subordinates who were not only not punished but went on to be promoted subsequent to the discovery of their indiscretions.

As I was completing this manuscript, in fact, I was advised by old friends inside the CIA of the name of the leading contender to be the next chief of CTC. The officer in question, a senior ops officer with many years of experience, is a legend within the CIA for his blatant sexual harassment and for a long string of brazen sexual liaisons with junior officers. During one of his prior tours as COS abroad, he effectively conducted an "auction" of incoming female junior officers, reserving to himself the right to "bed" the most attractive and then "granting" to members of his senior staff the privilege to pursue those he found less desirable.

Standards are not something you can trot out for show when convenient and then disregard when it would be painful to enforce them. Either you either live by them or they are rendered useless and meaningless. If tomorrow a senior agency officer were dismissed from service because of a sexual relationship with a subordinate, that action would reverberate worldwide in a heartbeat, and probably most such behavior would be modified immediately.

6. TOUGHEN TRAINING:

The Cold War is over. The long, static, almost ritualized contest in which both sides abided by a set of rules governing their behavior and their treatment of spies has concluded. Officers engaged in the collection of human intelligence in today's world are required to penetrate terrorist organizations, drug cartels, and the security services of despotic regimes that adhere to no internationally recognized standards of conduct. Once upon a time, if you were caught, the worst that would happen was that you would be sent home. No more. Now if you are caught you are likely to be killed, and you are probably lucky if that death is quick in coming. The possibility of extended torture and dismemberment is very real. Officers are now also expected to deploy to areas that for decades were not areas of operation. While we will continue to need people in advanced nations of the First World, increasingly, our officers are going to find themselves in tribal areas, the deserts of Central Africa, and the jungles of Southeast Asia. They need to be tough enough to deal with these challenges, both mentally and physically, and they need to have the skills required.

Case officers in a new OSS will need more than familiarity with firearms and self-defense. They will need to be experts in both. They should have substantial training in explosives, with particular emphasis on improvised explosive devices and terrorist methodologies. They should receive substantial training in survival, escape, evasion, and interrogation-resistance techniques. They should know how to hot-wire cars, pick locks, and defeat common electronic security systems. All of them, unfortunately, should have a thorough grounding in nuclear, radiological, chemical, and biological weapons. They should, in short, be able to handle themselves in a considerably rougher and less physically forgiving environment than that which characterized most Cold War deployments.

Language training cannot continue to be an afterthought. Officers who are to spend their lives abroad need to be truly immersed in the cultures where they operate. A good friend told me a story not so long ago about being at work in the CIA and providing a briefing to an outgoing deputy chief of station (DCOS) on the history of the nation to which he was being assigned. At the conclusion of the briefing, the DCOS, who seemed generally disinterested in the whole topic, made a point of bragging about how he spoke not a single word of the language of the nation to which he was being sent and that in his career he had avoided ever having to learn any language.

This cannot continue. Training cannot be a joke. Our officers need to be honed to a high level of competence in a host of skills if we are to have any hope at all of defeating our enemies.

7. INSTITUTIONALIZE STANDARDS OF PHYSICAL FITNESS AND MEDICAL QUALIFICATION:

Our officers are increasingly called upon to deploy to remote areas on short notice and to perform under extremely stressful and dangerous conditions. When I was deployed to northern Iraq prior to the 2003 invasion, my team operated without the benefit of support from any other element of the United States government. We were alone, surrounded by enemies and forced to fend for ourselves. We had no medevac. There was no rear area. Our evacuation plan in extremis was to proceed due north overland into Turkey. Part of that journey we could have made by vehicle, but a significant portion would have had to be negotiated on foot. Our route out would have taken us through some of the most rugged terrain in the world, likely in the dead of winter, and would have, just as a kicker, involved the improvised crossing of at least one river.

This kind of movement is only possible with a group of individuals who are in superb physical condition. Some of the individuals on the team fit that bill. Some of them were in passable condition. Others, frankly, probably would never have made it out. They were great people, and they did good work, but realistically, they had no business being deployed to northern Iraq under those conditions.

During our deployment, when things were at their most difficult and the possibility that we might have to extract ourselves overland the highest, I went with several of the SF personnel assigned to the team to recon the route out. I remember vividly, after many hours of overland travel, standing on the banks of the river we would have to cross and discussing with a senior SF warrant officer how he proposed to construct a rope bridge to get our team across. I think if there was anyone on the planet who could have pulled that off, it was probably him, but all I remember thinking was that if I had to bring my entire team out via this route and we were being pursued, a lot of people were not going to make it. There were simply some individuals assigned who could not possibly hope to measure up to the challenge.

We cannot afford to continue to operate this way. We have to put ourselves in a posture where all our officers meet certain minimum physical and medical standards and are deployable on short notice to remote and difficult locations. Exactly what standard should be employed is a topic for legitimate debate, but I would suggest that the physical fitness standards utilized by the United States Marine Corps are probably a good guide. You do not have to be a world-class athlete to pass a Marine Corps PT test; you just have to have the self-discipline to maintain a regular exercise schedule and to push yourself to maximize your potential.

8. MAKE IT THE ONLY GAME IN TOWN:

If you are involved in the collection of HUMINT, other than SF-type low-level source-type operations or double-agent CI ops, you work for the OSS. That does not mean you coordinate with the OSS or keep it informed or use it as a guidepost or any other such nebulous requirement. It means you are under the direct command and control of OSS, and the OSS owns your budget.

We have moved to a ridiculous system that allows virtually every organization in the United States government to stand up its own clandestine human-intelligence-collection organization and to send officers overseas. We are then expecting the chief of station, whose authority to control foreign intelligence collection is dwindling by the day, to somehow control this chaos. This is not a practical way to do business. It is at best inefficient and counterproductive. Quite likely, in the very near future, it is going to prove disastrous. We are going to have damaging diplomatic incidents overseas because officers of some organization other than the CIA were caught in the act of collecting intelligence, and the postmortem is going to show that the chief of station in that country either did not know about the operation in question or objected to it and was ignored. We are going to have incidents in which officers of organizations other than the CIA are captured, tortured, and killed, and the investigation afterward is going to show that their deaths were not inevitable but were a consequence of inexperience and lack of coordination. We cannot operate in a world where the left hand and the right hand do not communicate. Today's intelligence collection challenges are already daunting enough, even when we have our act together. There is no margin for error, and sloppiness and confusion will only lead to disaster.

My comments should not be misinterpreted. I am not saying that all the other intelligence officers outside the CIA should be put out to pasture. To stand up a new OSS, we are going to need all the help we can get, and we are going to need personnel from a whole variety of organizations. Within the Department of Defense, the Defense HUMINT Service contains a large number of fully trained collectors and operational support personnel. Such individuals also exist in other organizations and will need to be called upon. The OSS would not be the CIA with a different label on it. It will be a new, dynamic organization drawing on the full range of available talent and ability.

9. USE IT SPARINGLY, AND WHEN YOU DO, SUPPORT IT:

Stop viewing the use of a clandestine human-intelligence-collection apparatus as the cure for all ills. If there is no national policy and no one has a clear road map to an acceptable solution, it is quite possibly better that we do not get involved rather than that we ask a handful of intelligence officers to perform miracles and then feed them to the lions when they cannot. A clandestine human-intelligence organization is a valuable tool and one without which our nation would be in grave danger. It is not a cure-all, and the more it is looked upon as one, the more likely it is to become embroiled in political controversy. This unique capability should be reserved for those situations that demand it.

A new OSS cannot be used, as the CIA has been, as the private instrument of the president of the United States. It must be used, in accordance with the Constitution of the United States, to take actions on behalf of the United States government. The president is the commander in chief, but this does not translate into his having the unilateral discretion to involve the country in foreign entanglements and proxy wars without the support of the elected representatives of the people. In the future, when a president of the United States is confronted with the kind of situation Ronald Reagan faced in the 1980s, when Congress would not line up behind his desire to fight a guerrilla war against the Nicaraguan government, that president will need to either convince Congress to support him or accept that his desires will go unfulfilled. If he does not, and he chooses to direct the capabilities of a new OSS into an effort that does not have the necessary level of domestic support, he simply will have initiated the same caustic cycle of decay all over again.

By the same token the Congress of the United States cannot simply observe from the sidelines and then, when something goes wrong, spring into action to utilize the failure for crass political advantage. A new OSS would exist, like the uniformed armed forces, to protect the citizenry of the United States. Much must be demanded of it, but by the same token it must be supported. We cannot afford to continue to crush the careers of good men and women who have risked their lives for this nation simply because it makes good press and helps with reelection prospects.

As this manuscript was being sent to the printers, the country remained mired in a controversy over the use of enhanced interrogation techniques (EITs). The Speaker of the House not only remained committed to the necessity for the creation of a "truth commission" to get to the bottom of the debate over the use of EITs but also continued to assert publicly that she had been deliberately misled by the CIA and, further, that it was common practice for the CIA to mislead her.

I will not waste a lot of space on this topic here, as it is peripheral at best to the central thesis of this book. I do think it appropriate to note, however, that I think the average American would be staggered if he or she really understood how much time the Central Intelligence Agency spends up on Capitol Hill briefing the Congress of the United States. It is no exaggeration to say that there are many days when a lot of critical work is simply not getting done at CIA headquarters because the necessary personnel are all tied up with answering queries from congresspeople or testifying before one of several committees. Any implication that Congress is sitting off to one side, uninformed and unable to access critical information is simply wrong.

Most importantly, however, this debate over EITs is a perfect example of what we cannot afford to do any longer regarding the intelligence community. My position is and has been clear: We should never have used EITs, and I have serious doubts that they were ever really as useful as has been claimed. To the extent they were useful, I think we ought to be paying more attention to the question of why our only decent sources of information were detainees, not agents, operating inside al-Qaida. If we were doing a better job of collecting intelligence in the first place, we would perhaps not have found ourselves so dependent on interrogations.

In any event the issue has been resolved. The president of the United States has changed the policy: EITs are no longer used and will not be used in the future. Case closed; it is time to move on. Staging a witch trial for the purposes of political theater and currying favor with the extreme left of the Democratic Party is simply going to send us back into another destructive cycle of tearing apart our intelligence agencies. We have a lot of work to do. We remain at war. We need to move forward, and to do that we need an energized, focused, and aggressive intelligence community.

10. DEMAND RESULTS:

As noted above, we cannot do everything. We shouldn't try. The purpose of a new OSS would be to do those critical tasks that no one else in government service can accomplish. It may well be the case that officers of this organization can provide valuable insights into the pace of global warming and the workings of the economy of Burundi, but unless these in some way touch upon truly pressing national interests of the United States and we cannot get the information other than by clandestine means, someone else should do the job.

Once we have made a decision to employ the capabilities of a new OSS, we should then establish clear operational objectives for it and demand results. Too often in the CIA, vague representations that some sort of planning process is underway or a program is being "initiated" passes for progress. We do not have time for this. Donovan was not interested in reports from the field suggesting that someone was thinking deep thoughts about taking action at some point in the future. He wanted concrete reports explaining how many assets had been recruited, how many covert teams had been deployed, and how much intelligence had been collected. We cannot afford to be any less hard-nosed. We need to demand accomplishment and be prepared to do whatever is required to ensure that we get it. There can be no substitute for success.

We must create a culture that understands that objective, quantifiable results are a requirement rather than a rarity. During the long years of the Cold War, it became possible to frame everything in terms of subjective, long-term, fuzzy concepts that often defied efforts at measurement and evaluation. We cannot afford this continued "soft" approach to production.

I am not talking about numbers here. At various points in its history, the CIA has attempted to address the issue of results by instituting bureaucratic procedures, such as the counting of intelligence reports produced by each station. Predictably, in short order, chiefs of station all over the world were directing that four-paragraph intelligence reports be rewritten as four separate, one-paragraph reports in order to pad the numbers. The day when we could tolerate such nonsense has long passed.

What I am talking about are hard, quantifiable strategic objectives. During the Civil War, Lincoln wanted the Army of Northern Virginia defeated and Richmond taken. When General McClellan demonstrated he could not fulfill that requirement, he was replaced. In turn so were Burnside and Hooker, until Lincoln found Ulysses S. Grant, and the job got done. We need to have exactly the same kind of approach with a new OSS.

Establishment of strategic objectives for a new OSS is properly the job for a group of individuals with real, deep, current knowledge of the challenges facing the United States worldwide. Some of those challenges are well known to the population as a whole; some of the more long-term and perhaps significant challenges, however, are probably a lot more obscure and beyond the scope of my vision.

That said, I will go so far as to nominate some items that I think should be included on the list of things a new OSS would be required to accomplish and for which its leadership would be held responsible:

- Find Osama bin Laden, and capture or kill him.
- Destroy al-Qaeda.
- Penetrate the Iranian nuclear program to provide a complete, accurate, and current picture of the status of Iranian efforts and to ensure that there is no possibility we will be surprised by the acquisition of a nuclear weapons capability by that state. Provide a picture of this program in sufficient detail to enable the United States, should it become necessary, to strike and destroy this program in its entirety.

- Penetrate the North Korean nuclear program to provide the same level of visibility.
- Penetrate at a strategic level the military and political decision-making apparatus of both Russia and China to ensure that we receive advance warning in all cases of actions by those nations that may be detrimental to our national interest.
- Prevent the acquisition by any terrorist group of nuclear, radiological, chemical, or biological weapons.
- Penetrate the political and military decision-making apparatus of Pakistan to provide a clear picture of the stability of that critical nation.
- Penetrate the Pakistani nuclear program to provide complete clarity regarding the size of the program, the locations of all weapons, and the status of their security. As with the other nuclear programs referenced above, enable the United States, should it become necessary, to strike and destroy the whole of the Pakistani nuclear weapons capability.
- Penetrate the ranks of Hizbullah in preparation for the possibility of an eventual direct confrontation with that organization on the scale of our ongoing conflict with al-Qaeda.

As I noted above, these proposals are not intended to be exhaustive. Their purpose for inclusion here is to provide some concrete examples of what I mean by objective, verifiable results. Nowhere on this list is there any mention of a desire to have the OSS provide insight as to how the government of Malaysia may be attempting to vote at the next conference on global warming. Nor is there any reference to the OSS's telling us what the Spanish will do with regard to their pressing illegal immigration problem. We cannot afford the direction of precious, limited clandestine collection resources against a vast array of topics of significantly less than critical importance. The OSS should be expected to attack only the toughest targets and only those that truly threaten the national security of the United States. Against those targets, there should, ultimately, be only one inflexible standard—success.

11. DIVERSIFY:

There has been for some time a focus on the necessity for the movement of operations officers into nonofficial covers. This remains, however, still far too much a sideshow. The center of gravity remains staff officers, under official cover, serving abroad. This has, in fact, become the norm. It is expected that officers will typically serve the bulk of their careers under official cover; living a commensurate lifestyle; and subject, for the most part, to no threat greater than expulsion as a persona non grata. This has to change. We need to move to an organization in which officially covered officers are only one segment of a balanced workforce employing individuals posted abroad under a whole host of covers and communicating with headquarters via a myriad of technical and nontechnical means.

Along with the move to a much more diverse, less "official" posture, we need to substantially change the types of individuals brought on as clandestine operators. The Department of State has great success in recruiting individuals in their mid-twenties and then cycling them through a series of assignments to embassies and consulates in the course of a normal twenty- or thirty-year career. We cannot continue to depend on a similar set-piece recruitment and staffing process.

We need a certain number of individuals straight out of college or graduate school. To handle the challenges of operating in the current international environment, however, we increasingly need a much broader, more varied pool of recruits. We need former Army Special Forces operators, and we need international bankers. We need professors in Middle Eastern history, and we need nuclear physicists. We need native linguists, and we need archeologists, mathematicians, and commercial real estate brokers. We need individuals of Western European extraction whose families came to Plymouth on the *Mayflower*, but we also need first-generation Americans who grew up in Beirut, Delhi, or

Tbilisi. In short, we need exactly what the OSS had, a true cross-section of America in all its incredible, staggering diversity.

12. INCREASE COMPENSATION, AND TAKE CARE OF YOUR PEOPLE:

If you expect a man with a master's in Middle Eastern history to take on a career in which he will be faced with continuous threats to his life and will be required to raise his family abroad subject to all sorts of work- and non-work-related challenges, you are going to have to pay him well. No one is going to choose this lifestyle exclusively for money, but the fact remains that financial issues are significant.

It is one thing to pay an individual a GS-12 salary to live in a developed nation and work under official cover. While the cost of living in many such nations is going to be significant, the benefits and rewards of an officially covered lifestyle may still help retain many gifted individuals on the government payroll. It is quite another to take the same individual, deploy him to a Third World nation working terrorist targets and living on the economy as a third-country national businessman, and expect that a GS-12 salary will still be sufficient. If we want this new organization to do extraordinary things and to attract extraordinary people, we need to put the kind of money into it that is required. A new OSS will exist, ultimately, for only one purpose: to do those critical things that need doing and that no other government agency can accomplish. This cannot occur unless it attracts and retains the very best individuals possible.

Along with this increase in pay, we are going to have to take care of our people in other ways. The military is now finding out what happens when you pay lip service to supporting the family but, in fact, leave families to largely fend for themselves while the serving spouse does multiple tours in the combat zones. Stress fractures occur. Marriages fail. Suicide rates skyrocket.

We will suffer the same fate with a new OSS if we are not careful. A career in the DO is already death to most marriages. The pace of the work, the constant pressure, and the necessity for secrecy combine to kill a large number of relationships. An old instructor of mine once said that a DO officer was expected to die in the shower of a heart attack, while drinking gin, in his midfifties, estranged from his children, divorced from his third wife, and living with a woman half his age. Anyone who met a different fate, according to this instructor, was not working hard enough.

The pressure will be worse on personnel in a new OSS. They will not lie awake at night worrying about being expelled from the country in which they are serving or being passed over for promotion. They will lie awake wondering if they will live through another day. They will spend months undercover in dangerous, distant places with little or no ability to communicate with their loved ones. It will be a difficult, dangerous life, and the families involved are going to need all the help they can get to survive it.

The CIA often claims that it is one large family and that it takes care of its own. Once upon a time that may have been close to true. And every once in a while you see flashes of what it once was and, perhaps, in a different form, what it could be again.

Several years ago I was running a station in Asia, and one of my officers became very ill. Her only hope of survival was immediate transport to the United States by air ambulance. Working quickly, we got the officer to a hospital, laid on the flight, and then stood by monitoring her condition to ensure we did not lose her before we had a chance to get her on the plane.

As it turned out, it took many hours for the air ambulance to make it to our location. Our officer was in a local hospital all that time, and we needed to keep someone with her continuously, both for security reasons and to make sure that the local staff gave her the level of care she deserved.

I called for volunteers in the office to work two-hour shifts in the hospital until our ailing officer was transported out. One of the women who worked in a support capacity stepped forward. She said she would go and that there was no need for anyone else to take a shift. She would cover all the hours. She added that the stricken officer was her friend and her colleague and that she was not going to leave her side in any event until she knew she was on her way home.

She didn't do it for promotion or pay or a letter in her file. She didn't do it because of any personal reward she expected to receive. She did it because it was the right thing to do, and it would have never entered her mind to do anything less.

That is the spirit we are going to have to capture and build into a new OSS if it is going to face the challenges ahead.

13. KEEP IT INDEPENDENT:

The original OSS was besieged on all sides by bureaucratic enemies. In fact, after the death of President Roosevelt, those enemies were ultimately successful in convincing President Truman to disband the OSS. Donovan's bold experiment, which had accomplished so much, was shut down. It would take the onset of the Cold War and the stark reality of our lack of sufficient human-intelligence capability to convince Truman to reverse course and create the CIA.

Time and again during its brief existence, the OSS was able to get the necessary support only because of the direct connection of its leader, Donovan, to the president. When the FBI wanted to kill off the OSS at its inception, when the army wanted to bar the OSS from operating independently, when the State Department wanted to stonewall the OSS and refuse to allow the OSS in country, it was the direct connection to the president that saved the day. Without it the OSS could not and would not survive.

As I have noted earlier, a new OSS would not be the president's private plaything. He will not be free to use it whenever and wherever he chooses. That said, in the rough-and-tumble world of Washington politics, it will take serious support and leverage to keep the OSS from becoming mired down in the red tape, procedure, and arcane infighting that characterizes so much of the federal bureaucracy. Without a direct connection to the president, a new OSS will stand no chance against behemoths like the Department of Defense.

Whether or not we retain the position of Director of National Intelligence, I think, is a topic for another time and place. I remain unconvinced that the creation of that office and its attendant massive bureaucracy has really taken us in a positive direction. What is critical, however, is that the leader of a new OSS cannot be subordinated to the DNI and reduced to speaking to the top layers of the U.S. government through an intermediary. The issues a new OSS will confront are too vital and too time sensitive to allow for such a cumbersome arrangement.

14. MOVE NOW:

Richard Harris, who wrote one of the first overarching histories of the OSS, had this to say about the state of the CIA several years ago:

> *OSS was more than a little wacky. But underlying the wackiness was a sustaining "spirit" that had already begun to disappear in the 1960s when I served my federal peonage emptying classified wastebaskets. Without that spirit, what is left is a CIA that suffers from organizational hardening of the arteries. Even the best of secret servants would be hampered by a pervasive culture of inertia, lack of imagination, smug self-satisfaction, and that infectious curse of the bureaucratic mandarin, the incessant need to CYA: Cover Your Ass.*
>
> *Is such an agency, at age fifty-eight, prepared to deal with the unprecedented? Not merely the bogey of "terrorism" which is only the dread symptom of many and varied ills, but with cataclysmic problems of nuclear proliferation, religious fanaticism, superpower destabilization, even global medical and environmental threats? I think not.*
>
> *Can it then be changed for the better by organizational reshuffling and adding superlayers of bureaucracy? I doubt it.*[81]

Unfortunately, Harris was right. When Donovan was forming the OSS, he promised President Franklin Roosevelt that he would give him an international secret service staffed by young officers who were "calculating reckless" with "discipline daring" and trained for "aggressive action." We still have people like this, and amazingly enough, not a few of them are in the CIA right now, praying for a change that will set them free to do the work they know needs to be done.[82] That said, all the herculean efforts in the world by current CIA employees are not going to change the fact that the machine is broken, and it needs to be replaced if we are going to get back to the kind of creative and effective organization the OSS was.

Adding staffs, creating new coordination requirements, and turning the overall intelligence community wiring diagram into an even-more-tortured mess than it is already will not help. Memos, paperwork, PowerPoint presentations, and blue-ribbon commissions are not going to get it done either. We need to put aside form and process and get back to basics. Espionage is a tough, tough business. We need an equally tough organization to practice it.

We'd better hurry; the clock is ticking in a game we are playing whether we like it or not. It is a game we cannot afford to lose.

Endnotes

1 Patrick K. O'Donnell, *Operatives, Spies and Saboteurs* (New York: Kensington, 2004), xiii.
2 *COI Came First* (Internal Unclassified CIA Publication), 2.
3 O'Donnell, xiv.
4 O'Donnell, 49.
5 O'Donnell, 160.
6 Tom Moon, *This Grim and Savage Game* (New York: De Capo Press, 2000), 90.
7 Richard Dunlop, *Behind Japanese Lines* (New York: Rand McNally, 1979), 232.
8 O'Donnell, 313.
9 Gary Berntsen, *Jawbreaker* (New York: Crown, 2005), 307.
10 Richard Harris Smith, *OSS — The Secret History of America's First Central Intelligence Agency* (Guilford, CT: The Lyons Press, 2005), 4.
11 Steve Coll, *Ghost Wars* (New York: Penguin Press, 2004), 396.
12 Gary C. Schroen, *First In* (New York: Ballantine Books, 2005), 78.
13 Max Corvo, *OSS Italy 1942–1945* (New York: Enigma Books, 2005), 1.
14 Corvo, 46.
15 Corvo, 59.
16 Corvo, 120.
17 Corvo, 119.
18 I was, in fact, an Army officer on active duty from 1983 to 1987. I also served several years in the Reserves, both before and after this time.
19 The details of this process are extremely sensitive and will not be addressed here.
20 O'Donnell, 275.
21 Barry Rubin, *Istanbul Intrigues* (New York: Pharos Books, 1992), 252.

22 Rubin, 254.
23 Rubin, 255.
24 Elizabeth P. McIntosh, *Sisterhood of Spies* (New York: Random House, 1998), 147.
25 McIntosh, 150.
26 Will Irwin, *The Jedburghs* (New York: Public Affairs, 2005), 34.
27 McIntosh, 161.
28 Robin Bruce Lockhart, *Reilly: Ace of Spies* (London: MacDonald, 1967), 43.
29 Lockhart, 44.
30 O'Donnell, 267.
31 O'Donnell, 268.
32 O'Donnell.
33 Rubin, 164.
34 Irwin, 43.
35 Irwin, 47.
36 Corvo, 15.
37 Erasmus H. Kloman, *Assignment Algiers* (Annapolis, MD: Naval Institute Press, 2005), 11.
38 Kloman, 12.
39 *Report on the Guatemala Review* (Intelligence Oversight Board, June 28, 1996).
40 Tim Weiner, "Guatemalan Agent of CIA Tied to Killing of American," *New York Times*, March 23, 1995, 1.
41 Weiner, March 23, 1995.
42 *Report on the Guatemala Review*
43 *Report on the Guatemala Review*
44 *Report on the Guatemala Review*
45 *Report on the Guatemala Review*
46 *Report on the Guatemala Review*
47 *Report on the Guatemala Review*
48 Tim Weiner, "Senators Seek Legal Inquiry on CIA in Guatemala," *New York Times*, September 30, 1995.
49 Tim Weiner, "CIA Director Admits to Failure in Disclosing Links to Guatemala," *New York Times*, April 6, 1995.
50 Weiner, September 30, 1995.
51 Kermit Roosevelt, *War Report of the OSS, The Overseas Targets* (New York: Walker, 1976), 117.

52 Roosevelt, 127.
53 Roosevelt, 130.
54 Gregory A. Freeman, *The Forgotten 500* (New York: New American Library, 2007), xi.
55 Roosevelt, 130.
56 Roosevelt, 130.
57 O'Donnell, 88.
58 O'Donnell, 98.
59 O'Donnell, 131.
60 Moon, 203.
61 Lawrence E. Walsh, *Final Report of the Independent Counsel for Iran/Contra Matters* (Washington DC, August 4, 1993).
62 *Final Report of the Independent Counsel*
63 *Final Report of the Independent Counsel*
64 *Final Report of the Independent Counsel*
65 Roosevelt, 318.
66 Moon, 270.
67 Roosevelt, 319.
68 Moon, 273.
69 Moon, 274.
70 Moon, 276.
71 Schroen, 33.
72 Schroen, 34.
73 Schroen, 146.
74 Schroen, 159.
75 Berntsen, 314.
76 Berntsen, 315.
77 Memorandum dated September 6, 1941, from G. C. Marshall, Chief of Staff of the Army, Entitled "Undercover Intelligence Service."
78 Roosevelt, 1.
79 Dunlap, 259.
80 Dorothy Ringlesbach, *OSS: Stories That Can Now Be Told*, (Bloomington, IN: Authorhouse, 2005), 74.
81 Smith, xviii–xix.
82 Smith, 31.

Glossary

AFOSI (AIR FORCE OFFICE OF SPECIAL INVESTIGATIONS) A component within the United States Air Force, which conducts criminal and counterintelligence investigations.

AGENT Within the Central Intelligence Agency (CIA), this term is used to refer to an individual, usually a foreign national, who is recruited to spy for the United States and to provide intelligence. The Federal Bureau of Investigation uses this term to refer to its staff officers who conduct investigations and make arrests. The CIA does not use this term in that fashion.

AL-QAEDA A fundamentalist Sunni Muslim extremist group led by Osama bin Laden. Currently, the bulk of the leadership of this organization is based in the tribal areas of Pakistan.

ANSAR AL-ISLAM A fundamentalist Sunni Muslim extremist group composed primarily of Kurds. Prior to the last Gulf War, it controlled an enclave along the Iraq–Iran border. It has since ceased to exist under this name, although many of its members have been active in other Sunni extremist groups fighting against Coalition forces inside Iraq.

CASE OFFICER Also known as **operations officer.** These are the individuals within the Central Intelligence Agency who recruit spies and run operations. They are typically referred to in the mainstream press as "agents." The CIA does not use this term.

CENTRAL INTELLIGENCE AGENCY (CIA) The premier HUMINT collection agency within the United States government. Traditionally, the CIA has been divided into four directorates, which are each tasked with a separate function. The Directorate of Operations runs operations and collects intelligence;

the Directorate of Intelligence analyzes the information collected; the Directorate of Administration provides logistics, finance, and other forms of support; and the Directorate of Science and Technology provides technical support and expertise to operations.

COMMS Communications.

CONUS (Continental United States). This is the same term used by the U.S. military.

COUNTERINTELLIGENCE (CI) Operations directed against the intelligence activities of hostile nations. Sometimes these operations are defensive, in that they are focused on identifying enemy agents within organs of the United States government. Sometimes these operations are offensive, in that they are directed against the intelligence officers of hostile powers.

COUNTERTERRORISM CENTER (CTC) A bureaucratic entity within the CIA. CTC has responsibility for pursuit of all terrorist groups worldwide that are judged to pose a threat to the national security of the United States.

DEFENSE HUMINT SERVICE A clandestine military HUMINT collection service within the Department of Defense.

DETACHMENT 101 The first operational OSS unit; active primarily in Burma against the Japanese.

DI ANALYST An analyst working inside the Directorate of Intelligence. His or her job is to review all source intelligence coming in from the field and to produce disseminable pieces of finished intelligence, which are provided to policymakers and agencies of the U.S. government.

DIRECTORATE OF OPERATIONS (DO) As noted above, this is the component within the CIA that actually conducts operations overseas. Formally, the DO is now referred to as the National Clandestine Service (NCS). I have elected to ignore this relatively recent change in nomenclature, since it has typically been disregarded in the field by DO officers.

DIRECTOR OF THE CENTRAL INTELLIGENCE AGENCY (DCIA) The title given to the head of the CIA since the recent intelligence "reforms." This individual runs the CIA and does not control the overall community. Prior to the "reforms" the DCIA was known as the DCI, Director of Central Intelligence, and was considered the head of the community.

DIRECTOR OF NATIONAL INTELLIGENCE (DNI) Pursuant to the post-9/11 intelligence "reforms," the DNI nominally runs the entire Intelligence Community.

DIVISION/DIVISION CHIEF The Directorate of Operations of the CIA is divided organizationally into a number of regional divisions, which are responsible for operations in those corresponding areas of the world. The Near East Division (NE), for example, covers the Near East and South Asia. There are also other division-level-equivalent organizations, which are not focused on regions but rather on subject-matter issues. CTC is a good example of this, in that it is focused on terrorism worldwide. All the heads of these entities are considered division chiefs or the equivalent in rank.

DONOVAN, WILLIAM World War I war hero and founder of the OSS. A statue of Donovan, who was known affectionately as "Wild Bill," stands in the lobby of CIA headquarters in Langley.

ELINT Electronic intelligence. Intelligence acquired through the intercept of electronic signals.

GROUND BRANCH (GB) The paramilitary component within the CIA responsible for military-type operations. Personnel in Ground Branch are usually former military special operations personnel.

HALL, VIRGINIA Decorated OSS officer who served inside occupied France during the Second World War; considered by the Gestapo to be the single most dangerous OSS operative.

HUMINT Human intelligence; intelligence collected from human sources.

IMINT Imagery intelligence; most commonly, satellite photographs of targets of intelligence interest.

INTELLIGENCE COMMUNITY (IC) This is the group of sixteen separate intelligence agencies within the United States government. It is often also referred to simply as the Community.

LIAISON SERVICE A local security service in a foreign nation with whom the CIA maintains a cooperative relationship.

LOGISTICS OFFICERS CIA officers responsible for supply and logistics matters, both at headquarters and overseas.

MASINT Signatures intelligence; this includes the collection of a wide variety of different types of information, including telemetry from missile tests, measurements of radiation from nuclear weapons storage facilities, and collection of soil samples near chemical weapons factories.

NAVAL CRIMINAL INVESTIGATIVE SERVICE (NCIS) An organization within the United States Navy that conducts criminal and counterintelligence investigations.

NEAR EAST DIVISION (NE) The geographic entity within the Directorate of Operations that controls stations and bases in the Middle East, North Africa, and South Asia.

OFFICE OF MEDICAL SERVICES The office within the CIA responsible for employee health, physicals, inoculations, and so forth.

OFFICE OF SPECIAL SERVICES (OSS) Created at the outset of World War II to collect foreign intelligence and conduct covert action behind enemy lines; it was largely the brainchild of General William Donovan. The OSS was disbanded at the end of World War II as the result of opposition from the Department of Defense and the Federal Bureau of Investigation. Two years after the OSS was dismembered, President Truman signed the order creating the CIA.

OPERATIONS OFFICER See **case officer** above.

PATRIOTIC UNION OF KURDISTAN A Kurdish political and military entity that controlled roughly one half of the territory in northern Iraq prior to the Gulf War. The northern portion of Iraq, in the Kurdish areas, was nominally independent of Saddam Hussein and functioned for all intents and purposes outside the framework of the Baghdad government.

PERMANENT CHANGE OF STATION (PCS) This refers to a permanent transfer from one duty station to another. This is the same term used by the U.S. military.

POLYGRAPHER The person who administers lie detector tests. All CIA personnel are subjected to polygraph tests periodically. Assets are frequently tested as well.

REILLY, SIDNEY A British intelligence agent/officer of the early twentieth century. Reilly was an assumed name; he was born in the Ukraine and was the illegitimate son of a Jewish doctor.

SENIOR INTELLIGENCE SERVICE (SIS) In the context of this book, the Senior Intelligence Service is the equivalent within the Intelligence Community of the Senior Executive Service (SES). Officers in the SIS are general officer equivalents serving in civilian capacities within the Intelligence Community.

SIGINT Signals intelligence; intelligence acquired from the interception of electronic communications.

SITREP Situation report; a standard report provided to update higher command on the status of key factors such as personnel strength, casualties, the progress of an operation, and so on.

STATE DEPARTMENT The entity within the United States government charged with conduct of foreign relations. The State Department does not conduct clandestine or covert operations.

STATION A CIA office abroad, usually located in a city of a country. Subordinate offices within the same country are known as bases.

TDY Temporary duty; this refers to a transfer to a temporary duty station. Such a transfer may be for a few days or for many months. At the end of a TDY, an officer is expected to return to his permanent station of assignment. This is the same term used by the U.S. military.

TENTH SPECIAL FORCES GROUP A "Green Beret" operational group based at Fort Carson, Colorado; one of several U.S. Army Special Forces Groups.

WEAPONS OF MASS DESTRUCTION (WMD) Nuclear, radiological, biological, and chemical weapons capable of inflicting mass casualties. They include, but are not limited to, nuclear weapons, radiological dispersal devices, nerve gas, anthrax, and ricin. A significant number of terrorist groups around the world, including al-Qaeda, are known to have ongoing programs focused on the development or acquisition of such weapons.

Index

About the Author

Charles S. Faddis is a retired CIA operations officer. Prior to his departure from active service at the end of May 2008, he was the head of CIA's WMD terrorism unit. He served in Europe, South Asia, and the Middle East and spent most of his career running operations directed against terrorist organizations, WMD proliferation networks, and hostile regimes. Prior to joining the CIA in 1988, Faddis was a U.S. Army officer and a trial attorney. He attended the Johns Hopkins University and the University of Maryland School of Law, both in Baltimore, Maryland.

Faddis now lives near Annapolis, Maryland, with his wife Gina C. Faddis. The couple has four children, two of whom are still living at home. When he is not writing or running his own consulting business, Orion Strategic Services, Faddis enjoys sailing, winemaking, and traveling abroad. His next book, on homeland security, will also be published by The Lyons Press.